THE PLAIN MAN
LOOKS AT THE COMMANDMENTS

THE PLAIN MAN
LOOKS AT
THE COMMANDMENTS

by

WILLIAM PURCELL

COLLINS
ST JAMES'S PLACE, LONDON
1966

TO ALL THOSE WITH
THEIR LIVES BEFORE THEM

© William Purcell, 1966
Printed in Great Britain
Collins Clear-Type Press
London and Glasgow

AUTHOR'S NOTE

In the present temper of opinion, when traditional morality is so much under question, anyone who sets out to write even as small a book as this on an ancient body of rules for living, all but one of which starts with the words 'Thou shalt not', might fairly be said to be taking on a difficult task. That being so, it seems important to state, here at the beginning, why the task has been attempted at all.

It has been attempted out of a conviction that in these almost forgotten commandments there is still, as in an electric cable in an abandoned building, a strong current of truth running, and that this live current can be used to power an answer to the haunting question, left very much in the air nowadays, but still pressing in many departments of life, 'why shouldn't I?'

That question bears more heavily on the young than the old. They have their lives before them; their problems to solve. This book is dedicated to them, with affection and regard.

One thing has become very clear in the making of this book: that the great virtue of the Ten Commandments is not so much that they lay down the law as that they make one think. The questions at the end of each chapter are offered as helps in that process.

WILLIAM PURCELL

CONTENTS

FOREWORD

*by G. W. H. Lampe, Ely Professor of Divinity,
University of Cambridge*

To many people, including some Christians, the Old
Testament is unexplored territory. Except as the source of
some vaguely remembered stories for children, or as the
book of a series of lush film epics, it is unknown ground.
Not only unknown but distinctly uninviting; for it suggests
a joyless picture of a stern and jealous God who burdens
his creatures with arbitrary and restrictive prohibitions
and, whenever these are disobeyed, descends upon them
in wrath like a Victorian headmaster. At best it suggests a
grim religion expressed in a narrow and puritanical morality
embodied in negative rules and regulations: something very
alien, not only to liberal humanism but to the spontaneous
love, sympathy and compassion of Jesus Christ.

If this widely held notion of the Old Testament were
true, and not (as it is) a caricature, then it would be quite
right to say that it is the very opposite of Christianity.
For the New Testament presents us with a gospel, that is,
'good news'. In one aspect this is news of liberation from
legalistic religion. 'Legalistic religion' means, roughly,
the belief, which is still by no means uncommon, that a
large number of rules, including many laws of conduct,
have been laid down for us by God; that when we obey
or break these rules a credit or debit entry is, as it were,
entered to our account in a celestial ledger; that when
our file is sent for at the final reckoning a credit balance
will earn us the right to go to heaven while a figure in the
red will send us to hell.

9

Such a religion offers no good news. Law, if we think of it as a kind of examination leading to a certificate of acceptance by God, can do only one of two things: register our failure or else make us complacent towards ourselves and censorious towards others. The good news which Jesus and his followers tell us is that God does not deal with us on this sort of basis at all. We do not have to earn his love. On the contrary, God has accepted us without regard either for our achievements or our failures, and welcomed us as his own children. If we, for our part, are willing to accept this, we can be free men and women; for if we know that we are already loved, however good or bad we may be, we can be liberated from preoccupation with ourselves and set free to love, and do good to, other people for their own sake. 'We love,' said St. John, 'because he first loved us.'

If this news is not only good but also true, it follows that our moral conduct is in no sense a way for us to commend ourselves to God. It is rather the way in which we respond to the given fact that God has accepted us as his children: the way in which we behave because we know that we actually *are* people whom God loves. So Christian conduct is not determined by merely external rules but by inward disposition. There are in fact remarkably few detailed moral codes in the New Testament: perhaps none at all. What we find there, for instance in the Sermon on the Mount, is a series of thumbnail sketches of the sort of person that one will want, and try, to be if one takes seriously the given fact that God has put us into a right relationship with himself and with other people. One will not simply abstain from murder because it is forbidden by law: one will refrain even from insulting another person because one has come to see that he is a brother. Our only obligation (and it is far-reaching and compelling) is to trust in God's love for us and to love our neighbour.

Foreword

It may seem surprising that the Ten Commandments in the Old Testament are based on the same kind of good news which we can find in the New Testament. The preamble to the Commandments, addressed to the people of Israel, says: 'I am the Lord your God, who brought you out of the land of Egypt, out of the house of bondage.' This means that God rescued them from slavery and made them his own people without waiting to see if they would obey his laws or not. He did not save them as a reward for good conduct. On the contrary, he brought them out of their miserable plight before he had ever given them any laws. His laws came later; and their purpose was not to show Israel how to earn the right to become God's people, but to indicate the sort of response that was called for now that they already *were* the people of God.

Like the Sermon on the Mount, the Ten Commandments are not an exhaustive and detailed moral code. They offer a series of brief sketches depicting the sort of dispositions and motives which characterise God's people. The first four illustrate an attitude of trust in God and loyalty to him, in response to his goodness in rescuing Israel. The last six depict certain basic attitudes towards other people which follow out of a right relationship to God.

Canon Purcell asks in this book why even these very general and fundamental injunctions should be given. Is it not enough to know that our proper attitude to God is trust and loyalty and to our neighbour sheer love? In a sense it is, for all right conduct can be brought under these headings. But in practice we need to have these extremely general principles broken down. We must have certain guide lines to help us to apply them to real life and its problems: not a rigid code of detail, which would be inflexible, but guidance of a more specific kind than the general exhortation to trust God and love others.

It is probably true that the problem of road accidents

would be solved if every driver had a disposition to be careful and considerate. But to say this is scarcely helpful without some kind of highway code to indicate various specific ways in which carefulness and consideration may be applied. On the other hand such a code would frustrate its purpose if it tried to lay down detailed rules for every complicated situation that one might encounter. The driver has to exercise his own judgment within certain lines of guidance.

The Ten Commandments play a somewhat similar role. They indicate certain sample ways, of a basic kind, in which the moral attitudes proper to people whom God has accepted should be exercised. Disloyalty to God is ruled out, under four headings. Selfish aggressiveness towards others is similarly ruled out in six sample, but fundamentally important, instances. They are all quite general, and as Canon Purcell has shown, they cover a wide range of moral situations and problems within which we have to exercise our own judgment. They do, however, give enough guidance to save us from the impossible task of trying to play each and every situation purely by ear.

They are in line, both in their purpose and their content, with the 'character sketches' in the New Testament. Jesus both based much of his own teaching upon them and also revealed new depths of meaning in them when properly understood. In this book a highly interesting attempt is made to show, as is the case, that their meaning can profitably be related to moral problems which were undreamed of when they were first composed: to such questions as the making of nuclear weapons, the control of population, phoney advertising and lying propaganda. As guides to our conduct in such matters as these they are relevant and compelling; a fact which suggests that the ancients had a true insight into their authority when they imagined that they had been penned by the very finger of God.

Prologue

In the National Physical Laboratory, in carefully controlled temperature conditions, is a length of bronze with a golden stud inserted near each end. The distance between these studs is exactly thirty-six inches, or one yard. Maintained with this curious object is a platinum cylinder weighing, equally exactly, one pound. Both are inspected at intervals on behalf of the Standard Weights and Measures Department of the Board of Trade, and copies are kept at the Royal Mint, the Royal Society, Greenwich Observatory, the Palace of Westminster, and at the premises of the Department itself.

The purpose of this elaborate procedure is basically simple: to maintain standards by which objects in common daily use can, if necessary, be checked, thus preventing the chaos which could arise from the growth of varying opinions as to what in fact these units of measurement represented. An impossible situation would quickly arise if the matter were left to opinion, and all opinions were equally respected. Some might hold, for instance, that a yard should in modern times be twenty inches. Others, perhaps of a more conservative turn of mind, might favour thirty-six on the grounds of precedent. Others yet again might maintain that the matter was of little consequence, provided always that people were left free to make up their own minds. Clearly, this just would not do, any more than would differences of opinion as to which side of the road traffic should use. In other words, it is a demonstrable fact of experience that, in large areas of life, generally accepted standards, and at least some generally accepted rules, are necessary if confusion is to be avoided.

But how far does this principle reach? Does it, above all, extend into those areas of human experience where moral judgements arise, and where issues of what we like to call rightness and wrongness are involved? This is the great question looming behind so much of life today. Is there, in fact, any absolute standard to which we can still appeal when faced with any of the many forms in which the haunting question 'Why shouldn't I?' can present itself. The question matters enormously, even if an answer is difficult to find. To those personally concerned, it is of importance whether they are to marry a partner with an open mind on the subject of faithfulness or someone who believes that being faithful, in the sense of not generally sleeping around, is right. Either way, it is going to make a difference. And similarly, it matters whether people work with or for honest men, or for those who. untroubled by moral considerations, are prepared to sell them down the river whenever it suits their own interest.

Some moral judgement is involved in every human action of any importance, and always has been. The only varying factor is the form in which moral judgements present themselves. And with us, the fact of living in a world where science has so vastly extended both the freedom and the consequences of human action, the need for some such judgement is not less, but greater, and covers the whole range of behaviour. Is it right, or wrong, for instance, for men to make a doomsday weapon?

The trouble with moral judgements, however, is that they become very difficult unless there is in existence a standard against which the actions involved in them can be measured. Without an idea of rightness, wrongness can no more be evaluated than darkness can be identified without a knowledge of light. The theory is clear. But in practice is there, in fact, any body of moral law which, carrying absolute authority, and being meaningful in all ages and places, including the here and now, is strong enough to serve as a guide to how we should conduct ourselves?

The question is not new, and various attempts have been made to answer it. Men have often tried to regulate life by rules, and equally often succeeded only in arousing opposition. The answer to the moralists' 'Thou shalt not' very easily becomes a spirited and rebellious 'I will,' especially when the moralist has lost the power, as he largely has now, to frighten or intimidate. Thus in the field of sexual morality the threat of hell-fire and the probability of pregnancy might have had some effect in discouraging promiscuity. Yet even if they did—and the evidence is not impressive—the kind of morality thereby achieved would still suffer from a fundamental flaw in that it would represent a result achieved by the coercions of fear rather than by a willing submission of the heart and mind. Virtue can never be enforced, and the history of the many attempts to do so, from the severities of Puritanism to the social pressures of Victorian England, are not encouraging. Both led to backlashes of hypocrisy and rebellion worse, in many ways, than the excesses they sought to regulate.

Yet it remains true that all human societies need a code of some sort as a guide to the business of living. Indeed, all possessing vigour and purpose have one: only, it seems, in those not possessing these characteristics does the idea gain ground that no code is necessary. On the other hand, the stronger the sense of purpose the stronger, often, has been the sense of living to rule. So religious communities have had their codes—significantly often called Rules, like that of St. Benedict—and so also have the ostensibly non-religious. The standard of morality among the men and women of certain partisan units living in the forests of

15

eastern Europe in the second world war was a source of astonishment to western observers. Here, as in ancient Sparta, was to be found a rule of life harshly imposed, yet willingly observed because it was seen to serve the ends or purposes for which that particular society existed. This is not to say that such a severity is commendable—it may well be appalling and barbaric. But it is to say that respect for some kind of rule of life or code of conduct, whatever it may be, does seem to be a necessary part of any community life possessing coherence and purpose.

But we have not yet answered the question as to whether any body of moral law exists, carrying absolute authority meaningful for us now, and yet free of unpleasant overtones of fear and coercion. It is a difficult question, although one to which it is important at least to try and find an answer, if only because the consequences of not having one are grave. Those who cannot rule themselves end up by being ruled, in some way or other; which is only another way of saying that societies so libertarian as to be concerned only with the sacred right of everyone to do exactly as he likes have an unfortunate habit of succumbing either to their own internal weaknesses or to the assaults of more disciplined, if less civilised communities.

It is an old, old pattern of events. And almost equally old is the claim that only religion can provide the absolute values by which such internal moral decay can be prevented. But this claim needs critical examination. Religious belief is not the only foundation upon which a code of conduct can be based. The partisans based theirs upon shared loyalty to a common cause—defeat of the enemy: the Spartans upon obedience to the state. And many men of high principle, from the Stoic philosophers of the ancient world to high-minded agnostics of the present, have found, in a general desire to serve the common good, a moral basis for their lives of a quality which often compares, in terms of plain goodness, more than favourably with those of the ostensibly religious.

It is therefore an over-simplification to state that without religious conviction moral standards of any sort perish from the earth. That is just not true. But what do perish from the earth are moral standards which satisfy two very important conditions of effectiveness: that of being held to derive their authority not from man but from God, and, secondly, that of being changeless, of standing above the ebb and flow of argument, of being, in short, true for all people all the time, not just for some people some of the time. Moral standards of that heavyweight calibre are rare indeed. They cannot, by definition, be invented; they have to be discovered. And though respect for them may not necessarily prevent people from falling into all manner of sins against God and each other, yet it does at least make it possible for them to know when they are doing so. This is important; for the time for all of us to get really worried is not when the world becomes sinful—it always has been —but when the people in it begin to believe there is no such thing as a sinful world. An absolutist moral standard is at least a safeguard against that particular fate, just as the perfect yard measure is a safeguard against the chaos-producing situation wherein everyone might come to think, not that units of measurement were matters of opinion, so much as totally unnecessary.

Is there, then—and this is the third time of asking—in existence any body of absolute moral law of this nature? The answer is plain: there is such a body of moral law certainly in existence, but for the moment largely out of sight, like a piece of old-fashioned furniture not entirely thrown away, because of some sentimental value, but relegated to the attic, where it collects dust. Its name—a very famous one for a very long time—is the Decalogue, or Ten Commandments.

The Plain Man Looks at the Commandments

The reputation of the Ten Commandments was once very formidable indeed: since they had—as indeed they still have—all the credentials of a moral code standing above time and change: divine origin and authority, vast antiquity. So they had an important formative value for the life of the western world, influencing the framing of our laws, biting deep into the moral consciousness of generations. For in these commandments a voice like none other was heard, the voice of God himself, uttering those memorable words, *Thou Shalt Not*, and providing a solemn undertone to many an act of private decision and of public policy. 'What dost thou chiefly learn by these commandments?' the catechism asked. And the answer was 'My duty towards God, and my duty towards my neighbour.'

Once, especially following a notable re-discovery of them in Reformation times, they were brought by as many means as possible to the general attention—painted on the walls of churches, stamped on the minds of generations through the Catechism. Miles Coverdale's quaint version, which appears on page 156 at the end of this book, was a translation from the German of Martin Luther. Both were attempts at popularisation. The Book of Common Prayer to this day reminds the godparents in the baptism service that the child is to be taught the Commandments 'to his soul's health'. The Communion service in the 1662 Prayer Book required them to be said distinctly by the priest, 'and the people, still kneeling, shall after every commandment, ask God's mercy.' A similar ordinance of the Church of Scotland ruled that they 'be distinctly read by the minister immediately after the belief is said.' The Council of Trent, in a catechism prepared for use in Catholic churches, emphasised their great importance: 'Our ancestors have wisely reduced the whole force and system of the doctrines of faith to these four heads, the Apostle's Creed, the Sacraments, the Ten Commandments and the

Lord's Prayer.' Shakespeare was an infant of three when a government order required that 'the tables of God's precepts' be fixed in churches where everyone could see them, as no doubt he did himself. Thus, over a long period of time, in many parts of Europe and later beyond, one would often have been reminded, in Coverdale's words, of:

> . . . *the holy commaundements ten,*
> *Which God oure Lorde gave so strately,*
> *By Moses his servaunte, unto all men,*
> *Upon the hygh hyll of Sinai.*

Why, then, have they been to a large extent, as far as the present is concerned, pushed out of sight and mind? This is sometimes literally true: in many a church 'the tables of God's precepts'—and the Victorians were as fond of them as the Elizabethans—have been taken down or painted over. Nor are they heard, never mind taught, to anything like the same extent that was once the case. In the world in general it is as though there has been some quiet, almost sub-conscious assumption that a body of moral law which for many generations had a real grip on the conscience has become no longer serviceable. And since the purpose of this book is to offer an opportunity for looking again at these Commandments, and of asking whether in fact they are as obsolete as all that, it is important, here at the beginning, to be clear as to some of the reasons why, apparently, they have come to be thought so.

One of them is certainly to be found in the almost universal turning aside from any form of imposed moral authority which came, roughly, with this century. To be a rebel against any form of 'Thou Shalt not' is, of course, old hat by this time. 'Why shouldn't I?' has taken its place. But there was a time when to be rebellious against this sort of thing, and to be progressive, were necessary elements in being up-to-date. The antique world of Shaw and Wells is the place where the process can be seen excellently. 'Old-fashioned people,' said Mrs. Miniver in Wells's novel *Ann Veronica*, 'knew right from wrong: they had a clear cut, religious faith that seemed to explain everything, and give a rule for everything. We haven't. I haven't, anyhow. . . .' So it was with many others. And it must have been fun, and not very difficult, to demolish all those images of authority, ranging from God to heavy parents, and certainly including Moses and his Commandments, who were held to represent authority. The psychologist has helped, too, with the discovery that repression based upon authority can produce disastrous results. Naturally, this idea has proved very popular, and certainly should be included among the reasons why a moral code such as the Commandments, which at first sight seems to be wholly occupied with telling people what they ought not to do, has fallen upon evil days.

And then, too, authority itself in a whole variety of forms—military, political, scientific as well as religious—has time after time made a spectacular mess of things in this century. 'They'—the people in power, the people who ought to know—have far too often been found inadequate as the terrible events of this century have unfolded. The first world war began the process of exhibiting the clay feet of authority. The consequences of the murderous stupidities of that time are still with us. The lull between the wars expedited the de-bunking process, when authority in the form of statesmen and politicians proved quite incapable of meeting the political and economic challenges of the times. The second world war again weighed authority in the balance and found it wanting. And in the years since, scientific authority in its new guise as potential destroyer of the world has been shown to be yet another false God. And since the Commandments represent authority in the religious field, they have been involved in the common ruin of the idea itself.

Prologue

The Commandments stand or fall upon the question of their divine authority, being by no means all concerned, or even primarily concerned, with the relationships of man to man: but with the relationships of man to a God whose existence is assumed. The Commandments also presuppose —one may almost say take for granted—something about him—that he cares how human beings behave, and experiences a sense of injury done to the relationship between himself and mankind when their behaviour falls short of his standards. In other words, there is here presupposed a God whose very nature is on the one hand love and on the other hand righteousness.

This is the God, in fact, who spoke with Moses as a man speaks to his friends, but who, when asked to show his glory, 'passed by before him and proclaimed, the Lord, the Lord, a God full of compassion and gracious, slow to anger and plenteous in mercy and truth.'

What is more, these commandments proclaim principles of universal validity, which is one of the many reasons why they deserve now an unprejudiced examination by all concerned with sanity in human relationships. For covetousness is an evil in any society. Murder, theft, lying and adultery are destructive of the good life under any banner. These things are universal. Principles are needed for a proper ordering of all lives, not only of some.

But there is one other reason why the Commandments have faded from the scene. A change has come over much of Christian thinking since their great days—a change based upon the feeling that the law of Moses has been superseded by the teaching of Jesus, thus making the old prohibitions—the 'Thou Shalt Not' approach—no longer necessary.

Yet how true is this, in plain, unsentimental fact? To love the Lord thy God with all thy heart, with all thy soul, with all thy mind, and with all thy strength, and thy neighbour as thyself, is certainly Christ's way. It was still Christ's way, it may be observed, in the days when our fore-bears were insisting upon the great importance of the Commandments. The principle of love is the ideal answer to most problems of human conduct in any age. 'Love God, and do what you like,' as Augustine is reported to have said. 'Always treat others as you would like them to treat you,' runs the so called Golden Rule in St. Matthew. Yet the notion that unredeemed human nature is capable of living up to such an exalted standard without the stiffening element of a code of moral law is relatively new. It is also quite false, as any unsentimental look at the various motives and impulses which make us tick will render plain. But what we are principally concerned with here is not so much to prejudge these Commandments in any way, as to present the facts about them—largely nowadays for-gotten—so that we can reach some conclusion as to their present relevance or lack of it. Do they matter still, or don't they? If they are brought down from the attic, to which changes of taste and circumstance seem to have relegated them, how in fact do they blend with the dècor of modern living? One thing is certain: nobody can answer this question without having the evidence before him, no one can hope to find out what the Commandments have to say to him personally without first taking trouble to find what in fact they are saying at all, and saying now. And even that is not possible without the re-discovery of what in fact the Commandments are.

They could be called an attempt at Maker's Instructions for the conduct of human life, and are presented in the Bible as deriving their authority from a source above time and circumstance, and for that reason as eternally sig-nificant: absolute, not relative. Their birthplace is given in the most familiar of all accounts of their origin[1], as Sinai, a

[1] Exodus 19.18-20 and 20.1-18.

strange rock wilderness. The description of the event has marked elements of drama, as though the intention were, by investing the occasion with as much awe as possible, to give the narrative maximum impact.

And Mount Sinai was altogether on smoke, because the Lord descended upon it in fire: and the smoke thereof ascended as the smoke of a furnace, and the whole mountain quaked greatly.

And when the voice of the trumpet waxed louder and louder, Moses spake, and God answered him by a voice.

And the Lord came down upon Mount Sinai, to the top of the mount: and the Lord called Moses to the top of the mount: and Moses went up. . . .

And God spake all these words, saying, I am the Lord thy God, which have brought thee out of the land of Egypt, out of the house of bondage.

Thou shalt have no other gods before me.

Thou shalt not make unto thee any graven image, or any likeness of anything that is in heaven above, or that is in the earth beneath, or that is in the water under the earth.

Thou shalt not bow down thyself to them, nor serve them: for I the Lord thy God am a jealous God, visiting the iniquity of the fathers upon the children unto the third and fourth generation of them that hate me.

And shewing mercy unto thousands of them that love me, and keep my commandments.

Thou shalt not take the name of the Lord thy God in vain; for the Lord will not hold him guiltless that taketh his name in vain.

Remember the sabbath day, to keep it holy.

Six days shalt thou labour, and do all thy work:

But the seventh day is the sabbath of the Lord thy

God: in it thou shalt not do any work, thou, nor thy son, nor thy daughter, thy manservant, nor thy maidservant, nor thy cattle, nor the stranger that is within thy gates:

For in six days the Lord made heaven and earth, the sea, and all that in them is, and rested the seventh day: wherefore the Lord blessed the sabbath day, and hallowed it.

Honour thy father and thy mother: that thy days may be long upon the land which the Lord thy God giveth thee.

Thou shalt not kill.

Thou shalt not commit adultery.

Thou shalt not steal.

Thou shalt not bear false witness against thy neighbour.

Thou shalt not covet thy neighbour's house, thou shalt not covet thy neighbour's wife, nor his manservant, nor his maidservant, nor his ox, nor his ass, nor anything that is thy neighbour's. . . .

And all the people saw the thunderings and the lightenings, and the noise of the trumpet, and the mountain smoking: and when the people saw it, they removed, and stood afar off.

Here, clearly, is deliberate dramatisation on the part of a writer working centuries after the time of the event he seeks to describe. And equally clearly it is not, to say the least, at all probable, and for that matter is no longer intelligently maintained, that so sophisticated a code could have been meaningful to a primitive people or translated to them at such a time and in such a manner. There are even two biblical versions of the Commandments, that in Deuteronomy differing in certain significant respects from the narrative in Exodus. And behind both was an ancient and much shorter original. Yet, although the matter of their origin is confused and complex, as is the way with most ancient things, one truth stands out still as unmistakably as Sinai itself towered out of the desert sands— that the Commandments, however simple their early forms, however sophisticated they became later, were always seen as coming ultimately from God, and as bearing the stamp of his authority upon them.

If that be true, it means that what they say is true now. The great thing is to find what in fact they really mean for today, once the dust has been blown off them.

Necessarily, this means a critical look, a fresh look; but at the same time one which is prepared to search behind the outer form for the inner reality. A Scottish prayer book of 1637 summed up this matter well when it laid down that people should ponder the Commandments 'either according to the letter, or to the mystical meaning'; in other words, with a bit of imagination, care, and concern for the truth.

This is a path of enquiry not many of us nowadays have been along. So let's begin, and see what we can find at the earliest milestone along it, which is the first commandment.

I   One God

I am the Lord thy God. . . . Thou shalt have none other gods before me. Exodus 20. 2-3

There have always been many gods. There are now, although in the modern world they live in men's minds rather than in temples or sacred groves. There is the god of Self, always looking at his own face in a mirror, the god of Money, with a fistful of cash, the god of Social Status, with the built-in sneer. All have plenty of worshippers. What is more, there is a direct line of connection from them back to gods of earlier times—to those other deities who, in the sun-bright Mediterranean cultures of Greece and Rome, were thought to dwell on Olympus. And in another place and culture there were those primitive gods of whom Psalm 135 contemptuously declares, 'Eyes have they but they see not: they have ears, but they hear not.' Such were Milcom of Ammon, Chemosh of Moab, Asteroth of the Zidonians, and many others worshipped by the people of Israel in Old Testament times. And the connection between them is that men felt them to be worthy of worship. So it would be nonsense if the first commandment were claiming that there was only one God. But it is in fact claiming that there is only one worthy of worship—the great God above all, the God behind the ordered dance of the atoms, the God, too, of the moral law:

> *Judge eternal, throned in splendour,*
> *King of kings, and Lord of lords.*

There is nothing obvious about this concept. As a matter of fact it has always been easier for men to think of many gods than of this great, stark One. Primitive religion peopled the world with gods; saw them in trees, heard their chuckling in running waters, or their anger in the storm. It was an enormous advance in adult thinking to replace this childish many with one God supreme.

There are people who maintain that there is no God at all. Equally, there are many—and they have often included people of great integrity—ready to maintain there *is* a God, without wanting, or feeling honestly able to go further than that. But few appear to wish to argue about gods in the plural. We have all passed beyond that stage. Everywhere, the old gods are dead or dying, and new, psychological images of Self, Possessions, Position, Power, Sex and the like, taking their places. So the question of the great singular—the One God alone—still matters enormously because, as those who believe in him would claim, the whole meaning and purpose behind life depends upon the fact of his reality. Studdert Kennedy put it well, way back in the twenties: 'At its heart the world is not mad; but sane. That is the bare minimum of faith for man. If that goes, everything goes, and we can neither live nor think about life; but only take a long time to die.'

So the claim of this commandment is not that other gods do not exist, but that the true one stands alone, and will stand alone, in the mind and heart when the rest are abandoned. Once this first commandment is fully understood and so obeyed in spirit and in truth, then other gods fade from the consciousness. Indeed, this is what actually happened in the long centuries of development between the earliest version of the first commandment, which probably ran something like: 'Thou shalt not worship any other God but Yaweh,' and the exalted vision of the prophet Joel: 'Ye shall know that I am in the midst of Israel, and that I, the Lord, am your God and there is none else.'

The Old Testament is rich in accounts of how God

communicated with individuals at specified times and places. Abraham heard his voice, Isaac spoke with his angel unawares, Jacob saw in a dream a ladder between heaven and earth, Moses heard him not only upon Sinai but, long before that, in the ringing silence of the wilderness when a voice came from a thorn bush with the red evening sun burning upon it. And from then on in a line centuries long there are records of men similarly honoured, even though such encounters have always been exceptional.

'The old pagans had to choose between a brilliant, jangling, irresponsible, chaotic universe,' said Joy Davidman in *Smoke on the Mountain*, 'alive with lawless powers, and the serene and ordered universe of God and law. We modern pagans have to choose between that divine order, and the grey, dead, irresponsible, chaotic universe of atheism. And the tragedy is that we may make that choice without knowing it—not by clear conviction but by vague drifting; not by denying God, but by losing interest in him.'

Now an 'irresponsible, chaotic universe' is not a good place to live in. Let us look at this further. Sanity, in its widest sense—the built-in conviction that there is a meaning in things—depends upon the possession of a sense of order and purpose underlying all experience. It is a significant fact that one of the characteristic symptoms of some common forms of mental disorder is the loss of this very thing. The patient becomes disorientated, cut off from recognisable points of reference, like someone lost in a fog. So, however complex and difficult life may be, we have, if we are to make anything of it at all, to be able to feel a consistent principle at the heart of things. We can live with the knowledge that much of what we do doesn't make sense. What we cannot do is live with the knowledge that nothing makes sense.

The truth of this can be seen as operative over the whole field of human experience. It is, for instance, of critical importance to science. Without the basic assumption of order in that world, no principles could be established of any lasting significance, since they would lack the essential element of consistency, as is acknowledged by some scientists themselves.

'The scientist has a faith . . . which is reflected in the fact that he would never consider that an experiment begun on a Wednesday would yield entirely different results from one undertaken on a Friday. He believes in the orderliness of the universe. He stakes his shirt on his faith that everything happens in such a reasonable and well-ordered fashion that the same experiment will give the same result, whoever makes the observations, and wherever and whenever they are carried out. . . . If the contents of our universe did not behave in so regular and predictable a fashion no real scientific research would be possible.'[1]

A similar thought is expressed in loftier terms by Albert Einstein: 'You will hardly find one among the profounder sort of scientific minds, without peculiar religious feelings of its own. . . . His religious feeling takes the form of rapturous amazement at the harmony of the natural law. . . .'[2]

And as in the scientific field, so also is it in the realm of moral values: there has to be the sense of an unchanging point of reference before any universal value-judgements of goodness or badness, rightness or wrongness, can be made. There is an analogy here with the need of the scientist to be able to assume that, say (to quote Pilkington again), 'hydrochloric acid poured on limestone chips will always generate carbon dioxide, wherever the experiment be carried out,' and the need of Everyman to know that mercy and justice are good anywhere, and hatred and

[1] Roger Pilkington. *World Without End*. Fontana Books.
[2] Albert Einstein, quoted by C. A. Coulson. *Science and Christian Belief*. Fontana Books.

cruelty bad whenever and wherever they occur. Both assumptions require a background orderliness and consistency at the heart of things—an orderliness and consistency which can only come from one single point of origin. Both moral values independent of the ebb and flow of circumstance, and that faith in a basic principle of order which underlies all scientific research, may therefore be said to depend on, and indeed to stem from, the first commandment's concept of the one God rather than the many.

But it is in the personal life of men and women that its tremendous importance can most clearly be seen. Throughout history it has been an observable fact of experience that decay of the idea of God has led to a diminished sense of responsibility in the individual. Once the sense of accountability to God—the very essence of a religion based upon a personal relationship with him—has gone, the motivation for any conduct based otherwise than on self-interest has to a large extent gone likewise. Nor is the sense of personal accountability to God of importance only on the credit side of human conduct. It can work the other way, too. What else do we mean by the conscience? The sense of God is a check upon irresponsible action of all degrees. And it is when the sense of it has faded from the consciousness altogether that the drift sets in towards the bewildering, utterly insecure world of 'Why shouldn't I?'—a world which can easily arrive at the point of being unable to produce any particular reasons why any conduct whatever, however vile or anti-social, should be condemned. It is worth bearing in mind that the gas-chamber of the concentration camp was as much a product of the belief that anything goes in human conduct, so long as it serves some particular end, as the most seemingly trivial private peccadillo based on the same outlook.

Strangely, a multitude of gods seem to exercise no comparable force to the One. Polytheism—the worship of many Gods—has always been a-moral, and frequently immoral. What happened to the people of Israel when they emerged from the stern simplicities of the wilderness and got mixed up with the local deities of Canaan is a frequent theme of the Old Testament. 'They sacrificed unto devils, not to God: to gods whom they knew not, to new gods who came newly up, whom your fathers feared not,' says the indignant writer of Deuteronomy. The deep and abiding sinfulness of such actions, in which the scribes, centuries later, saw the explanation of many of the subsequent sufferings of Israel, lay at a deeper level. In the first place it devalued the whole idea of a God of moral righteousness to include him in the company of local gods who could be pleased by sacrifices or angered by their absence. He had sunk to the level, in fact, of the deities of the Graeco-Roman world of later centuries whose goings-on read like the gossip columns of a Sunday paper. And in the second place—and very importantly—it broke the bond or covenant made between the people and their God, out in the wilderness where the commandments were born, whereby if they kept his laws, he would keep his people.

'Know therefore that the Lord thy God, he is God, the faithful God, which keepeth covenant and mercy with them that love him and keep his commandments to a thousand generations.' Here is a thread of meaning which, like an electric cable, can be found running throughout the whole Bible. This is the drama of God and man; that man is forever breaking faith and having to be recalled to a timeless covenant of which the keeping of the divine law is a first necessity. It is a thread of meaning which leads also, in a startling manner, out into wide areas of life where its truth is acknowledged even when its starting point is unguessed at. When people shake their heads at the luxury, the selfishness, the blind materialism of so much of modern life, feeling in their bones that no good can come of it, what is really happening is that they have touched the live wire of this elemental truth that God requires, as the Bible puts it, 'righteousness in the inner parts,' in other words, responsible living.

So this first commandment is heavy with meaning still, though there are big questions left outstanding, which it does not itself answer, and was never meant to. What proof have we, for instance, that the God of whom it speaks, and which it assumes with the massive assurance of the monotheism which lies behind it, does in fact 'exist' at all? The question would have seemed a monstrosity to any thinker of the Judaistic world from which the commandments came. But it is a very burning one now. How are we to know that the whole concept of God is not man-made? Intellectual proofs, once fashionable, have a thin sound now. What are we to make, for instance, of the Ontological Argument (because a need for God is felt, therefore he must exist), or the Cosmological (that the universe must of necessity have a Maker), or the Argument from Moral Law (knowledge of right and wrong pre-supposed a source of moral values); and so on? Surely very little. Such exercises not only seem, but are, trivial in the face of the most momentous development of our times—the slow death, it sometimes seems—of the very idea of the divine as something beyond the self. An article in *Time* magazine put it well and honestly:

'In a sense, God—the personal omnicompetent deity of Christendom—has been dying for centuries. His lordship over the world has been threatened by every scientist who discovered a new natural law of organic growth, by every invention of man that safeguarded him against "act of God" disaster, by every new medicine that tamed a disease and solved another mystery of life. But it is the 20th century, the age of technological miracle, that has seen the triumph of the Enlightenment and the apparent banishment of God from the universe—even, thanks to Freud, from the human soul. Writing from his German prison cell in 1944, the anti-Nazi martyr Dietrich Bonhoeffer defined it as "the world come of age" in which "man has learned to cope with all questions of importance without recourse to God as a working hypothesis".'

If, then, this be true, what authority can lie behind, and what possible importance can attach to such a body of moral law as the Commandments? Significantly, the very article from which the passage comes was headed 'Christian Renewal,' and went on to develop the point that out of new perceptions of this God who has often in history seemed to die, but has always come to life again; especially out of a listening for his voice in the here and now, and out of a seeking to serve him in the secular world rather than in ecclesiastical ghettoes, a new sense of his reality will emerge.

'As usual, it was Bonhoeffer who best expressed the millennial hope for the coming of God's kingdom that lies behind the theology of renewal. "The day will come," he wrote from his prison cell, "when men will be called again to utter the word of God with such power as will change and renew the world. It will be a new language, which will horrify men, and yet overwhelm them by its power".'

It is, then, much too early to write off the moral authority of these commandments. But it is never too early, and certainly never too late, to try and look for their contemporary meaning beneath the dust of history. Meanwhile, two quite other arguments for the 'reality' of God—we have to use such admittedly loose terms until better ones are available—very different from the theoretical 'proofs' of a former day, may usefully be kept in mind.

The first is that people are experiencing God, in a bewildering variety of ways, as much in the present as the past. What is meant by 'experiencing'? A rough but true answer, judging by historical precedent, is that God is experienced whenever a change—of values, of direction, of effort—takes place in someone's life, which moves the individual away from purely personal concerns into areas of service and of dedication which uplift the whole tone of the life lived. A more solemn music is heard: a greater beauty perceived behind the face of common things. 'Lord, help me, teach me, come, enter within me. . . .' Prince Nekhlyudov prayed in Tolstoy's *Resurrection*, asking for release from the degradations of his former life. 'What he was praying for had happened already: the God within him had awakened in his consciousness. He felt himself one with him, and therefore felt not only the freedom, fulness and joy of life, but all the power of righteousness.'

This is the perpetual miracle of God breaking through, and is the most convincing testimony to the reality of the divine that there is. The men behind the commandment knew this experience—the electric shock of contact with God. And since no one who has received an electric shock feels disposed to question the existence of electricity, so the Bible does not raise the question of the existence of God, being concerned always more with his actions and attributes.

The second 'argument' for the reality of God is the evidence of what happens to peoples and societies when he is ignored. All the old evils of a crazy world of many gods then come creeping back, so that once again men feel at the mercy of blind chance, alone in a wide and empty universe, made all the more terrifying by their own powers of destruction. And if this is not a fair picture of our present situation, what is?

What sort of a god is this God of the first commandment? The very word, it has been sometimes said, represents a kind of empty frame into which we can put any likeness we wish.

This is perfectly true. It is very easy to have a wrong picture of God, including a childish one. And quite a number of people in every age have fallen for the temptation of putting themselves in the frame and worshipping what they saw there. Yet the Bible has a clear enough answer to this question. 'He hath showed thee, O man, what is good,' says the prophet Micah, 'and what doth the Lord require of thee, but to do justly, and to love mercy, and to walk humbly with thy God.'

In other words, he is above all else a *moral* God; one who looks for righteousness, and from whom justice can be expected and to whom their opposites—immorality, un-righteousness, injustice—are abhorrent. What is more, he is not, again in a phrase of Studdert Kennedy's, 'a staring splendour, like the sun,' but a God who cares about what happens to men and women. These could be said to be his fundamental characteristics, and it can be seen at once how distinct is the picture which emerges from anything else in mankind's attempts to portray the divine. And certainly he is also a God who acts and speaks, in history and in life, as the writers of the Bible were never tired of pointing out. When they wanted to speak of the reality of God they pointed to what he had *done*. So it is very much in character that the author of the Epistle to the Hebrews, writing to commend God's latest and greatest act, should say: 'When in former times God spoke to our forefathers, he spoke in fragmentary and varied fashion through the prophets. But in this final age he has spoken to us in the Son whom he has made heir to the whole universe.' And that is the specific-ally Christian answer to this question. The God of the first commandment is reflected in Jesus. 'Anyone who has seen me has seen the Father,' was how he put it, and that is the portrait which Christians ever since have sought to put into the frame.

Yet the full meaning of the command: 'Thou shalt have

none other gods but me' does not emerge with the dramatic force latent in it until we take a closer look at some of the alternatives. What, in fact, are these 'other gods'? The second commandment, looked at closely enough, can lead to quite a lot of interesting answers.

SOME QUESTIONS ABOUT THE FIRST COMMANDMENT

1. To the question 'Does God exist?' would you answer Yes, No, or Don't know?
2. What difference to life do you think the answer makes?
3. 'We can live with the knowledge that much of what we do doesn't make sense. What we cannot do is live with the knowledge that nothing makes sense.' Do you find this true?
4. Do you think moral values—standards of rightness and wrongness and the like—are important?
5. What do you feel they should be based upon?
6. Does it matter if they change from time to time?
7. 'Once the sense of accountability to God has gone, the motivation for any conduct based otherwise than on self-interest has gone likewise.' Is this true, in your opinion?
8. What, to you, is the most convincing argument for the existence of God?
9. Many today feel themselves at the mercy of blind chance. Do you find any connection between this and decay in the idea of God?
10. Do the discoveries of science necessarily work against belief in God?
11. Do you think God speaks to people today?
12. Can you recall times in your life when you felt the need of God?

One God

SOME THOUGHTS ON THE FIRST COMMANDMENT

The Greatness of God

The greatness of God is infinite; for while with one die man impresses many coins and all are exactly alike, the King of Kings, The Holy One (blessed be He) with one die impresses the same image of Adam on all men, and yet not one of them is like his neighbour. So that everyone ought to say: 'For myself is the world created.'

The Talmud: Sanhedrin

The Instinct towards God

The heart has its reasons, which reason knows not, as we feel in a thousand instances.

It is the heart which is conscious of God, not the reason. This then is faith: God sensible to the heart, not to the reason.

Blaise Pascal (1623-62): mathematician and man of letters

The Goodness of God

Upon the whole, there is a kind of moral government implied in God's natural government: virtue and vice are naturally rewarded and punished as beneficial and mischievous to society, and rewarded and punished directly as virtue and vice. The notion then of a moral scheme of government is not fictitious, but natural; for it is suggested to our thoughts by the constitution and course of nature.

Joseph Butler (1692-1752): philosopher and bishop

37

Duty towards God

And what doth the Lord require of thee, but to do justly, and to love mercy, and to walk humbly with thy God? *Micah 6. 8.*

Hear, O Israel: the Lord our God, the Lord is One: and thou shalt love the Lord thy God with all thine heart, and with all thy soul, and with all thy might.

Deuteronomy 6. 4-5

Religion and Atheism

It is true, that a little philosophy inclines man's mind to atheism; but depth in philosophy bringeth men's minds about to religion: for while the mind of man looketh upon second causes scattered, it may sometimes rest in them, and go no further; but when it beholdeth the chain of them, confederate and linked together, it must needs fly to Providence and Deity.

Francis Bacon (1561-1626): philosopher and essayist

God Everywhere

God is in the water, God is in the dry land, God is in the heart. God is in the forest, God is in the mountain, God is in the cave. God is in the earth, God is in heaven. . . .

Gouind Singh: Sikh

We praise Thee, O God, we acknowledge Thee to be the Lord. All the earth doth worship Thee: the Father Everlasting. *Te Deum Laudamus (about* A.D. *410)*

II Too Many Gods

*Thou shalt not make unto thee a graven image, nor the likeness
of any form that is in heaven above, or that is in the earth beneath,
or that is in the water under the earth. Thou shalt not bow down
thyself to them nor serve worship them; for I the Lord thy God
am a jealous God. . . .*   *Exodus 20. 4-5*

Let us be quite clear what we are looking for. We are looking for meaning in this commandment here and now, which
is the only justification for looking at it at all. And undoubtedly the first glance is unpromising: it doesn't seem
to contain anything relevant: graven images are not among
the world's preoccupations, and the itch to make them does
not afflict many.

The picture dramatically changes, however, when we
look, not outward to the world, but inward to our own real
interests in order to find the things, the images, the am-
bitions, the desires, the motivations which in fact we do
worship in the sense of giving them the best of our time and
energies. And if, as a result, we find that some, or even
many, are in fact false images of the good life, then it
could be that the search for the meaning of this commandment leads, after all, to truth—even to home-truths—about
ourselves of very considerable importance.

The worship of the false in any form is idolatry, and that
is precisely what this commandment is about. 'Thou shalt
not bow down to them, or worship them,' it says, speaking
of its 'graven images.' But it can be put another way. 'Thou
shalt not give respect to, or sell yourself body and soul to,
any of the images of the wealth or status, or pleasure

seeker which happen to be the rage at any given moment.' Objects of veneration come in many shapes; they can be graven in stone; they can be graven in the mind. The meaning of the commandment, which is concerned not with form but with falsity, is not affected in either case. It therefore follows that it is surprisingly heavy with meaning now, when the very word 'image'—the image of this, the image of that—takes on new life as part of the vocabulary of modern living.

What images of the highly desirable or the very important do we in fact make? There are so many, and most are so subtly inter-related, that there is danger of confusion. But at least we can select four—*Money, Self, Status* and *Pleasure*—see how they work and what they do to us. One thing should be said immediately: none of this particular quartet is necessarily wholly evil. Money has its necessary place in the scheme of things; some regard for Self is part of living; some regard for Status perhaps may have connections with an honourable sense of personal dignity; Pleasure may help us to find savour in life. In all cases it is the worship of them, enslavement to them, the bowing down and worshipping of them, which leads to trouble.

The *Money* god is very much a case in point. Traditionally his name is Mammon. The word in fact means 'money' and has been found on the tomb-stones of Phoenician traders of an age long before Christ was saying 'Ye cannot serve God and Mammon!' So he is a very old god, this one, and a very attractive one, too. For money can so obviously do so much that it is difficult not to conclude that the good life is in fact summed up in the possession of it. Money—the means of exchange—is as much a necessity of life as the spear or axe to primitive man. It gets things: food, clothing, warmth, transport, shelter. So it is important, and those prepared to deny the fact have usually been either those with too much of it, or those wishing to borrow some. But the concentration of mind, the surrender of body and soul to the getting of it, in other words the worship of Mammon, is another matter. Paul, as usual, spoke the truth when he wrote to his young disciple, Timothy, 'The love of money is the root of all evil things. And there are some who in reaching for it have wandered from the faith and spiked themselves upon many thorny griefs.'

Why is this so? It is important to be precise here, since many of the traditional condemnations of wealth have quite clearly been biased. Thus political condemnations of it have not infrequently owed much to the understandable animosity of the have-nots for the haves, notwithstanding the obvious truth—easily demonstrable from the history of philanthropy—that the possession of money does not necessarily betoken social injustice. And similarly, religious objections to wealth—a frequent phenomenon down the ages—have sometimes arisen from hostility to personal indulgence of any kind, and especially of those which money can buy, as things inherently unholy.

The real dangers of the inordinate love of money—those 'thorny griefs' St. Paul spoke of—are of quite another order. The main one, beyond any doubt, is that it *distorts value-judgements*, inevitably and naturally. Once money is enthroned as the be-all and end-all of existence everything else, including life itself, is seen in terms of it, so that the price of a thing looms larger than its value. The difference between the two is made plain by the problem which often faces young people starting off in life in an affluent society. Which sort of job are they to choose: the well paid, or the socially useful? Here is a value-judgement straight away. And because of the state of our values (almost all of them those of a money-worshipping society), the socially useful—the teacher, the nurse, and so forth—are usually the least rewarded in terms of money. So all the pressures upon young people starting out in life are likely to be towards selling them the idea that to go for the money is the sensible thing, however much they may feel in their hearts the desire for a stronger and more challenging motivation. 'Where there is no vision the people perish.' This is as true now as ever, and the sourness and staleness of a society whose primary interest is money is already afflicting our own.

Mammon worship is inevitably self-defeating: the more money we have, the more we come to need. That expenditure rises as income increases is one of Parkinson's laws. At the same time money values themselves decline—a thing which is happening now to many currencies. The old story of King Midas has an oddly close application here. Asked by a god what gift he most desired in the world, he chose the power of turning everything he touched to gold. But the gift turned out to be undiscriminating: his food turned to the metal, so that he could not eat, and his child, when he embraced her, became lifeless at his touch. So, life becoming impossible, he had to beg for the gift to be revoked.

Of course, economic circumstances such as ours, in which production of more and more goods is accomplished by progressive decline in the value of the money with which to buy them, create a climate for the religion of Mammon so favourable as almost to bring a smile to his usually stony face. So his devotees grow feverish as they always have done, and anxious, and fundamentally unhappy, sometimes without knowing it, because they are missing, in their service of the god, so many of the good and simple things of life, including time to sit back and wonder what on earth it is all about, this 'getting and spending, laying waste our powers' 'A man's riches ought to avail to the ransom of his soul, not to its destruction. And a treasure is a ransom, if a man use it well. On the other hand it is a snare, if a man know not how to use it. What is a man's money to him but a provision for his journey? Much is a burden, a little is useful.' So wrote St. Ambrose. But such wisdom is anathema to Mammon who demands now, as he always has done, all the heart and soul and mind and strength of his devotees. They must think money, talk money, love money for its own sake, evaluating everything in terms of its cash value. It was a deep insight which made Milton, when he wrote of Mammon as one of the rebellious angels, at once beautiful and dangerous, show him as one who was more interested in the fact that the heavenly pavements were made of gold than in anything else.

> *For e'en in heaven his looks and his thoughts*
> *Were always downward bent, admiring more*
> *The riches of Heaven's pavement, trodden gold,*
> *Than aught, divine or holy, else enjoyed*
> *In vision beatific.*

So this is a dangerous idol, this Mammon. He has also, because of the kind of civilisation which has developed in the western world, perhaps a larger following than any other. Today's constant talk about money is a tribute to his powers. His image sits enthroned in millions of minds, and it is a useful experience to look into our own, and see if he is there also.

Self certainly is, because the very existence of this god is intertwined with the instinct of self-preservation. So completely self-less people are rare indeed. But, as with money, the trouble here arises when personal interests come first in all things—when, in fact, 'looking after number one' is exalted to the level of a religion, in the sense that self becomes an object of worship. Here again is a distortion of values. In a society where 'getting on'—becoming richer, more important—is regarded as success, and the opposite as failure, a keen eye for self is regarded as one of the marks of a shrewd man who knows his way about in the world.

But there is a catch in this particular form of idolatry—

43

the worship of self carried to excess. *It is destructive of the power to love*, a dark truth which has been known for a long time, as another old legend, the tale of Narcissus, tries hauntingly to make plain. Narcissus was a beautiful youth, and very aware of the fact. A nymph, falling in love with him, died of grief when it was not returned, Narcissus being too pre-occupied with himself. Nemesis, goddess of retribution, she who carried in ancient mythology a whip in one hand and scales of justice in the other, as a punishment made him watch his own reflection in a pool, whereupon he became so enamoured of it that he gradually pined away of a love which could have no outreach, no fulfilment, because it was focused in the self. 'It is a poor centre of a man's actions, himself,' Francis Bacon wisely said long ago, and that is as true now as ever: but the place to look for the truth of it, if we are going to look at all, is in ourselves.

Another false god whose cult leads to distortion of value-judgements is the extraordinary idol of *Social Status*. This mean little god—mean more than dangerous, but still capable of causing much unhappiness—is the deity who decides who is 'in' and who is 'out'; who 'up' and who 'down'. He is the god, among other things, of class distinction, a very odd social phenomenon of much complexity. Some kinds of speech please him, some do not; some kind of clothes gratify him, some do not. Certainly, the cult of status is crazy, and it is easy to smile at it. But its evil lies deeper; it is basic to the kind of thinking which evaluates people not in terms of their kindness, goodness, courage, generosity and the like—the eternal verities—but in terms of position in the social scale. So the danger of this particular idol worship lies in the *falsification of human relationships* to which it gives rise.

Pleasure, another of these false gods which can be found enthroned in the mind, may be less intrinsically perilous, pleasure being concerned essentially with the ephemeral

44

and the passing. The danger here is of *trivialisation of life* rather than distortion of truth. Even so, trivialisation is a serious enough matter, since man has but the one life to live; and to devote most of it to the pursuit of passing enjoyments at the expense of learning a little wisdom, doing a little good, and at least trying to make the world, even by the minutest fraction, a little better for our having been in it, is to miss much. Of course, any blanket condemnation of pleasure is suspect. As with some of the traditional hostilities to wealth, the view that pleasure is in itself sinful, as though belief in God and a capacity for enjoyment were mutually incompatible, has done immense harm. Nor does it work out well in practice, if we may judge by the examples of rigorists down the ages. Even so, the notion that 'having a good time' can ever serve as an adequate blueprint for the good life is a dangerous one, and likely to become far more so, for when vastly increased leisure is a social fact—which is well on the way to happening—it will also become a social problem if the pursuit of pleasure is seen as the only alternative to work. The implications of this go deep indeed. For technology to create for the many what hitherto the many have never had—much greater freedom from what the poet Philip Larkin calls 'the toad work'—and then to fill the hours thus left available only with the pursuit of the ephemeral, is to do more than trivialise life; it is to place massive powers of life-shaping in the hands of the pleasure merchants, the entertainment and mass-communication agencies. After all, keeping the many amused while the few, or the élite, get on with the job of ruling them, is one way of organising human affairs. They knew that in ancient Rome when they provided bread and circuses. But it could scarcely be called a way consonant with human dignity or with a high sense of the importance of the individual personality. And, as with Mammon worship, so with Pleasure worship; the more it is indulged in, the more is required for satisfaction. Thus idolatry is self-defeating, largely because, like Mammon and Self and Status worship, it is basically false. The evil consequences which follow can be seen as giving significance to the words with which this second commandment closes: 'I the Lord thy God am a jealous God, and visit the sins of the fathers upon the children unto the third and fourth generation of them that hate me, and show mercy unto thousands of them that love me and keep my commandments.' In other words, the evil consequences of idolatry are cumulative, and the opposite is equally so.

And now here the complex trail towards the meaning of this commandment leads back to the beginning of it all. If the warning it contains is against the creation of false images of God, what in fact is the true one? The attitude of the Jews on this vital matter was unique, being nothing less than that no image of God was permissable at all. Not surprisingly, this anti-image passion of theirs greatly intrigued many non-Jews in the ancient world and was the cause of an odd incident in the year 63 B.C. when a group of high-ranking Roman staff officers might have been seen striding up the marble steps leading to the great porch behind the altar in the Temple at Jerusalem. They talked as they did so, looking around them with alert curiosity, their voices coming clear across the silence. The Temple was deserted. Jerusalem itself had fallen; there had been a massacre of Jews, and their king was a prisoner. The civil war which had caused this military intervention was over. And now, matters being thus satisfactorily concluded, it was possible for the General commanding, together with his staff, to devote a little well-earned leisure to the sights and curiosities of the historic place which had thus fallen to their arms.

The Temple, of course, was a must. Famed throughout the ancient world, its inner splendours were forbidden to the uncircumcised. Beyond the Court of the Gentiles it was death to any non-Jew to pass. Beyond the Court of the Women no female could pass. Beyond the great porch, between whose colonnades the soldiers moved, only those of priestly function could go. For there was the Holy Place. And behind that was the heart and centre of the Jewish world, the Holy of Holies. As the visitors, having passed through the porch, paused for a moment to look down the length of marble floor, they saw a curtain upon the further wall shrouding the ultimate mystery—the place where the Jews were believed to keep their God.

The party, led by their General, Pompey, had come to solve the puzzle as to what the God of the Jews looked like. They themselves, as Romans, were used to images. In statuary and mosaic, their cities and temples, even their houses, abounded in them. But nobody had ever seen one of the Jewish God. Pompey leading, the group moved forward. But when the curtain was pulled aside there was nothing there. The Holy of Holies was an empty space.

The phenomenon might have seemed inexplicable; but in fact it had powerful historical reasons behind it. The anti-image passion of the Jews, often carried to remarkable extremes—there was a Jerusalem riot in the time of Pontius Pilate when his military escort carried their standards, bearing imperial emblems, into the holy city— had been reached after hard experience of what they saw as the dangers of idolatry to a true concept of God.

At their dim beginnings, the Hebrews, living among peoples who, after the manner of primitive religions in all ages and places, made images of their gods, did the same. Jacob set up the boulder as an object of veneration in the place where he had his dream of the ladder between heaven and earth. The brass serpent Moses was said to have had made in the wilderness was an image. So was its replica, kept in the Jerusalem temple for generations until it was cleared out in the course of the reformation under Hezekiah. By that time, by the usual inevitable process, it had become an object of veneration, like the boulder in Bethel centuries before. This thread runs through the whole of the Old Testament; sometimes this, sometimes that ruler or kingdom was 'made to sin' by allowing or encouraging some form of idolatry. So Moses was furious with Aaron for permitting the golden calf, and 'Jeroboam the son of Nebat made Israel to sin' by making two of them, it having become quite common by that time for Yahweh, the one God, to be worshipped in the form of a bull.

Those who chronicled all this, it has to be remembered, were looking backwards in history, and seeing the subsequent sufferings of their people as somehow explained by their actions in the past. And among those actions, a falling away from the one true God, high in his righteousness, that same God with whom Israel had made covenant, loomed very large. The nation had begun to go downhill, it seemed, from the time when it had lowered its religious standards in order to practise easy and attractive idolatries. There was another thing, too: the Babylonians, into whose hard-faced, sophisticated civilisation a number of Hebrews had been carried off when Judah was conquered in 537 B.C., were great image worshippers. We can maybe get some idea of how the experience of Babylon hit these godly Jewish deportees by imagining what the impact of a city like, say, Reno, Nevada as it is now, would have been like upon the inhabitants of mid-Victorian Aberdeen. Idolatry and moral decadence, it seemed, were curiously, even menacingly, inter-related. Small wonder, therefore, if centuries later, by the time Pompey strolled with his staff into the Holy of Holies and found it empty, the Jews had that horror of idolatry which set them apart from all other peoples of the ancient world.

Too Many Gods

That horror was based on two hard pillars of truth: that once men make images of God they start to worship them; and that the images they do make, being generally trivial, lead away from a true concept of the one God who, as Paul wrote, 'alone possesses immortality, dwelling in unapproachable light. No man has ever seen or can see him.'

It is an elemental human need to worship something, and it is fatally easy to worship the false. And once worship of the one true God, invisible, righteous, eternal, be abandoned, the cult of little gods creeps in, as it did with the Jews among the fertility deities of Canaan, as it does with the new images—Money, Self, Status, Pleasure and the like—of our civilisation.

What is more, any representation of the divine in terms of imagery—material or mental—leads, time and again, to the ultimate rejection by critical minds of the idea of God at all. Many a man has been 'put off religion' by the paltry images of God he finds religious people sometimes have. Superstition and ignorance are the natural by-products of idolatry in any form, and eventual contempt for the whole business is usually the end-product as knowledge comes to shed its light into this murky corner of human experience. So a major cause of the decay of religious faith in many ages and in many lives has been an inadequate image of God. Intelligent people in the Graeco-Roman world were laughing at the gods of Olympus long before they lost their hold, largely for that reason, upon the popular imagination. The critical minds of the Reformation in another world and another age, found it necessary to repudiate, among other things, the abuses which had grown from the crude idolatry which had come to deface the religion of Christ.

So 'the old man in the sky' picture of God—an image deriving ultimately from the idea of a flat earth—has done much to devalue the currency of spiritual truth. So also has the image of a God somehow and somewhere outside the physical universe become difficult for people in an age of space exploration, so that the search now is for God within other dimensions of experience. 'The final psychological, if not logical, blow delivered by modern science and technology to the idea that there might literally be a God "out there" has coincided with an awareness that the mental picture of such a God may be more of a stumbling block than an aid to belief in the Gospel.' So wrote the Bishop of Woolwich in *Honest to God*. The fact is that any attachment of a temporal image to the idea of God is dangerous, and always leads to a cutting down of the divine to human size. The image comes to be worshipped rather than the God whom it is held to represent. The result is idolatry, which is what the second commandment is talking about—and is talking about relevantly now.

The only concept which triumphantly survives the erosions of time and the extending boundaries of human knowledge is that represented, therefore, by the mysterious emptiness of the Holy of Holies, a reminder of the fact that:

> *We limit not the truth of God*
> *To our poor reach of mind*
> *By notions of our day and sect,*
> *Crude, partial, and confined.*

SOME QUESTIONS ABOUT THE SECOND COMMANDMENT

1. What do you consider the most popular image of the good life today? Money, Self, Status, Pleasure?

2.
> *The dearest idol I have known*
> *What e'er that idol be;*
> *Help me to tear it from thy Throne*
> *And worship only thee.*
>
> (William Cowper)

What is your particular 'dearest idol'?

3. How important to you is money?
4. In your view what, if anything, is wrong with putting self-interest first?
5. How do you value others: by what they have, or by what they are?
6. How high do you rate pleasure?
7. What do you think to be the real meaning of idolatry—the worship of false gods—now?
8. 'Whatever we may accept with the top of our minds, most of us still retain deep down the mental image of "an old man in the sky".'

>   (Bishop of Woolwich in *Honest to God*)

    Why, in your view, has such a picture of God become inadequate nowadays?
9. What would you put in its place?
10. Can you think of any instances where an inadequate picture of God leads to an inadequate faith?
11. Why do you think the Jews were against having any image of God at all?
12. 'It is an elemental human need to worship something.' Do you feel this to be true?

SOME THOUGHTS ON THE SECOND COMMANDMENT

The Old Man in the Sky

It were better to have no opinion of God at all, than such an opinion as is unworthy of Him.   *Francis Bacon*

The Need for Submission

The submissive instinct is as truly instinctive as any other, and demands recognition in a life of perfect self-realisation. We must know how to be abased.

J. A. Hadfield: psychologist and doctor

The imagination enlarges little objects so as to fill our soul with its fantastic estimate, and by a rash insolence belittles the great to its own measure, as when it speaks of God. *Blaise Pascal*

The Dangers of Self-love

He who hates not in himself his self-love and that instinct which leads him to make himself a God, is indeed blinded.

Blaise Pascal

Pluck out self-love as with the hand you pluck the autumn water-lily, and you will set your heart on the perfect path of peace. *Buddhist saying*

A True Instinct

It cannot be that the instinct which has led to the erection of cathedrals, and of churches in every village, is wholly mistaken and misleading. There must be some great truth underlying the instinct for worship.

Sir Oliver Lodge: 1851-1940

Idolatry in the Past

Certain philosophers once asked the Jewish elders at Rome: 'If your God has no pleasure in idolatry, why does he not destroy the objects of it?'

Too Many Gods

'And so he would,' was the reply, 'if only such objects were worshipped as the world does not stand in need of; but you idolaters worship the sun and moon, the stars and the constellations. Should He destroy the world because of the fools that are in it?' *The Talmud*

Idolatry in the Present

Money
Silly people think that money commands the bodily goods most worth having. *St. Thomas Aquinas: 1225-74*

Self
The foolish man is full of selfishness; he toils day and night, greedy for wealth, as if he will never grow old, or die.
Jainist saying

One suffers most who is most selfish. *Taoist saying*

Pleasure
A life of pleasure is the most unpleasing life in the world.
Oliver Goldsmith: 1728-74

Final Word
The first step of wisdom is to know what is false.
Ancient Latin proverb

III What's in a Name?

Thou shalt not take the name of the Lord thy God in vain, for the Lord will not hold him guiltless that taketh his name in vain.

Exodus 20. 7

Let's be clear of one thing straightaway: This commandment is concerned with far weightier matters, with more mysterious and portentous affairs altogether, than casual profanity. Swearing might be anti-social, like any other form of verbal diarrhoea. It is certainly, as a habit, very old: camel drivers in the world Christ knew probably cursed their animals in the name of God. It is even an interesting habit, in the sense of being an off-beat commentary upon the power which the name used is felt, even if subconsciously, to possess. For that matter swearing itself is, if coolly examined, a curious affair altogether, having quite a lot to do with word-magic and belief—unconscious this time—in the power of a curse. But it is still not the primary concern of this third commandment.

What is at stake here, what the commandment really is concerned with, may best be seen by looking closely at an occurrence which happens daily in any court of law—the taking of oath. A witness is called, and as he enters the box the clerk hands him a card. It bears the words, always in the same form: 'I swear by Almighty God that the evidence I shall give shall be the truth, the whole truth, and nothing but the truth.' From then on; from the moment of repeating them, the witness is legally 'under oath,' and a special importance attaches henceforth to what he says, and a special penalty—the price of perjury—is incurred by him if what he says is knowingly false.

What does the court think it is doing? A short answer would be that it is seeking to surround the giving of evidence with every solemnity possible, as a means of safeguarding its truth. But there is in fact a greater depth of meaning involved. The words: 'I swear by Almighty God' are highly significant. To swear an oath by that name has been for centuries regarded as the highest guarantee of truth. Obviously, the validity of such a guarantee depends ultimately on the respect, awe, reverence—what you will— with which those using the name in such a context regard it. To lie under oath is perfectly possible. To swear by Almighty God without giving the matter a thought is equally so, and no doubt is done daily. But neither fact diminishes the true importance of the oath. Even so, if the question related only to legal procedure it might be of but limited importance. Yet in fact it goes very much further. The question of trust in the public dealings of men touches life at many points, and it is precisely the question of trust which is involved here; trust based upon not using words and promises lightly; trust based upon the conviction that there are some things so sacred that they must be neither devalued nor betrayed. Once that goes, much goes. Hidden away at this point, incidentally, is the curious fact that a man is untrustworthy to the degree in which he holds nothing sacred; the truth of which statement becomes more obvious the more it is thought about. Who wants to have dealings, unless it can be avoided, with anyone whose code of conduct is limited to the conviction that anything goes so long as he can avoid being found out? The point was well, if accidentally, made in a P. G. Wodehouse story in which a man was playing golf with his solicitor, and, detecting him stealthily lifting his ball in a bunker when he thought no one was looking, took all his business away from him next day. The implication is clear: he who cannot be trusted to keep the rules in private is at least likely to be shaky about keeping them in public.

But what is, in the last resort, going to strengthen anyone in keeping the rules in private? A passage in Exodus gives a clue:

'If a man deliver unto his neighbour an ass, or an ox, or a sheep, or any beast, to keep, and it die, or be hurt, or driven away, *no man seeing it*; the oath of the Lord shall be between them both, whether he hath put his hand to his neighbour's goods; and the owner thereof shall accept it, and he shall not make restitution' (Exodus 22. 10-11).

Here again the implication is clear: there is no guarantee other than a sacred oath—one taken in the name of God—between the owner of the cattle and the man in temporary charge of them, that the latter is speaking the truth when he says one of them was lost through no fault or dishonesty of his. No one could see what happened, because no one was there. Only the oath stands as guarantee of truth, and so long as both parties honour it, there need be no suspicion between them.

The trail of meaning here leads straight back to the commandment. Any court of law placing witnesses upon oath in the customary manner is in reality, even if unknowingly, performing an action of great antiquity, and making a pre-supposition of much significance. It is causing someone to swear by a name; and it is pre-supposing a God who exists as an invisible witness of human actions. A closer look at both action and pre-supposition uncovers some truths which are important yet often obscured.

Name-magic, in the first place—which is involved in swearing by a name—is tied up with the very stuff of human experience. To be on christian name terms with someone presupposes an intimacy of relationship. A man who can go round a works, or a school, or any other collection of people, and address individuals by their names, is often held to be demonstrating one of the first principles of good-leadership—that of knowing his people on a level of intimacy. By his knowing their names and by their knowing his name, there is somehow established between them a *rapport* which would not otherwise be possible. The sense of injury, or of insult, which can come from the forgetting of a name by someone who ought to know it is the converse of the same thing. In the biblical creation story, it was by naming the creatures in the Garden of Eden that Adam established dominion over them. Similarly with us; our names identify us. Without them, we are nothing. There is another consequence of this: possession of another person's name gives the possessor, in some strange way, a power over him, in the sense of having, as it were, a way into his personality. Someone hailed by his name will turn, and smile or frown as the case may be; but he will at any rate react in a personal manner. And the fact that it is the mere calling of the name which causes this response gives to the possession of that name its extraordinary—in the true sense of more than ordinary—importance. If, then, such a reaction can derive from the possession of a human's name, how vast must be the consequences of possessing and using the name of God! In essence, this is the thinking behind the third commandment, and much else in the Bible.

It makes sense, for instance, of such otherwise mysterious incidents as Jacob's wrestling. All one night, by the side of a stream, and quite alone, Jacob wrestled with a strange nocturnal visitor. With dawn, they drew off from each other:

'And he said, let me go, for the day breaketh. And he said, I will not let thee go, except thou bless me. But he said unto him, What is thy name? And he said, Jacob. . . . And Jacob asked him, and said, Tell me, I pray thee, thy name. And he said, wherefore is it that thou dost ask after my name? And he blessed him there. And Jacob called the name of the place Peniel: for, said he, I have seen God face to face and my life is preserved' (Genesis 32. 26-30).

This is not something of interest only in the field of comparative religion. For possession of someone's name does in fact, as we have seen, place us in a special relationship to the owner of it—a relationship of intimacy to which knowledge of the name is in some strange way the key.

Thus it begins to be apparent why to possess the name of God, above all to use the name of God, entails a heavy responsibility. It presupposes, and leads on to, a degree of intimacy. So gravely, in fact, did the Jews of old regard this that they shied away from using the name of God at all, preferring to use a synonym or substitute. Even that— as though it were radioactive—had to be treated with care. Elaborate ceremonial precautions were laid down even for the scribe who, in the course of copying the Law, might encounter the name. He was required to be attired in the full-dress uniform of his office, and to disregard interruption while the business of copying out the synonym for the Holy Name was in hand. Behind all this loomed the continual consciousness that to use the name of God was somehow to call up the presence of God. Here again, is something very old, very strange. 'Where two or three are gathered together in my name,' says Jesus in St. Matthew's Gospel, 'There am I in the midst of them.' So, if to use the name of God meant calling up the presence of God, how fearful was the offence to anyone with a sense of reverence of doing so unadvisedly, lightly, or wantonly! To use God's name vainly is to insult him. Joy Davidman put it well when she wrote, in *Smoke on the Mountain:* 'The third commandment is . . . like the sort of warning you see around power plants: Danger—High Voltage!'

What is involved in the whole business—and this is where the contemporary relevance of this commandment today lies—are the weighty matters of trust as between man and man, relationships between man and God, and personal integrity in a man himself. The first—trust—depends ultimately upon the value which can be attached to a pledged word. All men of goodwill and even common sense can surely agree on this; for here is yet another of the many points at which the broad principles of honest living and the God-focused injunctions of the commandments coincide. We are all affected by the disappearance from the world of the basic principle of trust. And that principle comes down, surprisingly enough, in the end to the feeling that every man has a responsibility outside himself and acts under the eye of a witness greater than himself—a witness, moreover, who is interested in the truth. This is a feeling deeply embedded in human experience. In the dignified words of Ecclesiastes: 'Be not rash with thy mouth, and let not thine heart be hasty to utter anything before God: For God is in heaven, and thou upon earth: therefore let thy words be few. . . . When thou vowest a vow unto God, defer not to pay it; for he hath no pleasure in fools: pay that which thou vowest. Better is it that thou shouldest not vow, than that thou shouldest vow and not pay' (Ecclesiastes 5. 2, 4-5).

Naturally, it is always possible to swear to tell the truth, the whole truth, and nothing but the truth, and still be a liar and a cheat. Even the best things can be abused. Yet it is still true that the ultimate safeguard, and indeed the only safeguard of all honesty, of all justice, and of all fair dealing, is to believe that, even if we can hide things from other people, we cannot hide them from God.

A too narrow interpretation of that last word is quite

disastrous here, and has done as much as anything to discredit this extremely important idea of accountability to a standard of judgement larger than self-interest. As was noted earlier, an inadequate picture of God leads all too easily to a progressive devaluation of the principles associated with divinity. So long as we are content with the child's eye view of God as an all-seeing eye jealously watching what we do, and ready at any moment to condemn, it is not surprising that we should grow out of it and past it. But to have a strong sense of an inner censor, of a personally accepted and respected code of conduct, is another matter altogether. Many have this sense. The feeling of disquiet which comes from an action which, even if the world knows nothing of it, seems to outrage this code, is a testimony to its reality. And, when this common fact of experience is pondered upon, it becomes clear that the sense of, in a strange way, 'being observed,' of living in the presence of someone or something 'from whom no secrets are hid' is both very widespread and dependent upon the connection that this 'other,' this someone or something, while dwelling within us, is yet greater than us. The man of principle is essentially one who knows why he has dishonoured himself, because his inner voice tells him so. To ignore this inner voice is, in a very real sense, to 'take God's name in vain.' And beyond that lie the terrifying possibilities latent in a situation where people have no principles at all, no sense of an inner censor, no sense of reverence for the greater than themselves. Almost any evil becomes possible then, from petty immoralities to the fearful cruelties of man to man with which this century in particular has abounded.

In essence, then, this commandment is concerned with perjury, the telling of lies under oath, the being a liar and a cheat, or a scoundrel in general without thinking it matters so long as no one finds out. The framers of the commandment swore by the name of God because they believed the reality behind that name to be about the most sacred thing there was.

'Thou shalt not swear by my name falsely, neither shalt thou profane the name of thy God,' is one of the commandments in Leviticus, and it is significant that it is placed between an admonition against stealing and lying and one against fraudulent dealing. The third commandment, as we have seen now, is intimately concerned with the whole matter of honesty in personal dealings. And though it may not be immediately apparent how such an application arises out of the injunction not to use God's name in vain, nor out of any realisation of the sanctity of that name, the relevance of the whole thing does indeed emerge when it is considered how much, how very much, of the day-to-day transaction in ordinary life depends upon a man's word being his bond. It is very doubtful, to take one instance alone, whether the intricate business conducted by banks could last for a day without the underlying assumption that, on the whole, people mean what they say when they pledge their word, spoken or written.

This seems a long way from those simple words, 'Thou shalt not take the name of the Lord thy God in vain.' But the connection is unmistakable. 'The Lord will not hold him guiltless that taketh his name in vain,' can soon seem to be true enough in the light of the consequences which follow from the breakdown of mutual trust.

The fact is that all those actions which we perform as in the eye of an invisible witness—and anyone who looks frankly at the workings of his own conscience will know them to be many—are actions performed, or promises made, or resolutions taken, or promises given, *as in the name of God*. That name is consequently devalued when there is little or no integrity of purpose behind such undertakings.

Nor is that all. God's name can be 'taken in vain' in a

whole variety of ways, and few there are who do not do so from time to time. Religious people, in particular, are frequent offenders, using the name with a familiarity which can only arise from a deficient sense of awe. The contrast between what people say in this context and what in fact they do has often been noted.

For some comfortable congregation to sing

> *Thy Kingdom come, O God,*
> *Thy rule, O Christ, begin:*
> *Break with thine iron rod*
> *The tyrannies of sin*

without having the slightest intention of doing anything themselves about it, is an empty use of big words. The makers of the third commandment would have called it taking God's name in vain, and they would have been right. And, similarly, to speak much of moral issues— the challenge of race prejudice to the Christian conscience, for instance, or the harsh facts of world hunger—without having some personal action to show as proof of real, rather than merely verbal involvement, is to be open to the same condemnation.

But, in the end, what it all comes down to is whether, in the last resort, there is anything deep down within ourselves which we hold sacred—so sacred that we are not prepared to talk of it lightly or use it as a convenience. The old Jewish copyist who would not work on a scroll which contained the sacred name until he had had a bath was expressing an elemental and timeless truth—that it is well to revere something we know is greater than ourselves.

SOME QUESTIONS ABOUT THE THIRD COMMANDMENT

1. 'I swear by Almighty God . . .' Why do you think witnesses in a court of law are asked to use these words?

2. Do you agree that the less things a man holds sacred, the less he is likely to be trustworthy?

3. What things do you hold sacred?

4. What do you feel about using God's name in swearing; that it is wrong, in bad taste, or does not matter?

5. Do you feel offended when people forget your name, or get it wrong? If so, why?

6. The Jews of old avoided the use of God's name because they respected it so much. How do you feel that contrasts with our usual practice?

7. What other motives, beside self-interest, have weight with you when deciding on any particular course of action?

8. 'Even if we can hide things from other people, we cannot hide them from God.' Do you feel that to be true?

9. Do you think it matters, either way?

10. 'Thou shalt not swear by my name falsely. . . .' Can you think of any example of this actually happening?

11. How far do you think 'having a conscience' depends upon the idea of God as a witness of our actions?

12. What, to you personally, does 'taking God's name in vain' really mean?

SOME THOUGHTS ON THE THIRD COMMANDMENT

No swearing at all

You are not to swear at all—not by heaven, for it is God's throne, nor by earth, for it is his footstool.

Matthew 5. 34

The Plain Man Looks at the Commandments

The Meaning of a Name

Almost the only statement about the Hebrew names of God which would command general acceptance from modern scholars is that their original meaning is unknown. The general terms, *'El* and *'Elohim,* may possibly be connected with the idea of 'strength'; of the epithets, *Shaddai* and *'Elyon,* the latter means 'lofty'; the personal name *Yahweh,* is explained in the well-known passage in the Book of Exodus (3. 13-14) either as 'He is' (*i.e.* 'becomes') or 'He will be' the suggestion apparently being that the God of Israel actively manifests Himself as, or will show Himself to be, what He is.　　　　　*H. Wheeler Robinson*

God Must have a Name

To attempt to worship a God without a name, is to attempt the impossible. . . . Religion is falling in love with God; and it is impossible to fall in love with an abstract God, He must have a name. . . . Even to call Him the 'Good Father' is not enough; for the meaning of goodness is not fixed. . . . 'Our Father' is not really the name of God, the name of God is 'Jesus.' The Christian faith says boldly to mankind, 'Come, let us introduce you to God. His name is Jesus, and He was a Carpenter by trade. Hold out your hand, and He will take it in His.' The intellectuals may rail at the picture-book theology of the common man; but picture-book theology is the only possible clothing for real religion. . . . The Universal Beauty must create a picture before I can say, 'I see.' Universal Goodness must perform an action before I can say, 'I love.' Universal Truth must have a biography before I can say, 'I understand.'
　　　　　G. A. Studdert Kennedy

What's in a Name?

The Importance of a Name

Primitive man regards his name as a vital portion of himself and takes care of it accordingly. . . . The North American Indian regards his name not as a mere label, but as a distinct part of his personality . . . and believes that injury will result as surely from the malicious handling of his name as from a wound inflicted on any part of his physical organism. . . . Some Esquimaux take new names when they are old, hoping thereby to get a new lease of life. The Tolampoos of Celebes believe that if you write a man's name down you can carry off his soul with it.

Sir James George Frazer: The Golden Bough

A Prayer to the all-knowing God

Almighty God, unto whom all hearts be open, all desires known, and from whom no secrets are hid: cleanse the thoughts of our hearts by the inspiration of thy Holy Spirit: that we may perfectly love thee, and worthily magnify thy holy name.   *Book of Common Prayer*

IV Day off a Week

Remember the Sabbath Day, to keep it holy. . . .   Exodus 20. 8

Abstention from work, just like abstention from food and sex for certain periods, is an ancient principle at the heart of a good many disciplines. There is plenty of evidence that it is also a thoroughly good idea in itself, a factor in sensible and healthy living. And abstention from work is, basically, the concern of this commandment, the real point at which it is still meaningful for today, in spite of the fact that the dust lies thicker on it than possibly on any other. For what is at stake here is another principle, that of a weekly pause in the headlong rush of life, and of what we do with that pause.

It is easy enough to do nothing with it, of course. But in that case, if we are to be honest with ourselves and with the whole subject, the truth must be faced that the average Sunday as we now it know has become quite often something of a bore. 'Sunday is a time when you regret, remember, make plans and resolutions,' said a Sunday paper article recently, 'The trouble with Sunday is that to-morrow is Monday.' But there is more to it than that: there is something big and important for life itself, or at any rate for the way we shape it, hidden away in this whole business of Sunday. But neither the bigness nor the importance nor even the interest of the matter, which is very considerable, can be come upon without, at the beginning, getting rid of some prejudices.

The first, the most strongly held, and yet almost certainly the weakest in the face of the facts, is that we have somehow today been emancipated from a tyrannical Sunday of yesterday.

The essence of this argument is that Sundays were so ghastly in our childhood that we have become determined to make them very different now. 'Sunday can mean late breakfast, a chance to linger, unshaven, and read the Sunday newspapers. A day when time can be wasted; but which in the wasting induces feelings of guilt,' said the same article, 'because, for most of us, Sunday when we were young meant routine and duty: church or chapel, best suit, clean shoes, tight collar, one or two hymns we really did enjoy, and then the ordeal of the sermon; prayers, when we sometimes covered our eyes with our hands, sometimes stared, wondered who God was.'

But unless the writer was in or beyond late middle age, this cannot have been the case. Except for the elderly, no one living in the sixties of this century can have encountered Sunday observance of that kind as a generally accepted social convention, except in parts of Wales, or Scotland. The thing has been dead too long for that. For almost anybody of forty or under, the Sundays of their childhood must have been well within the period when social pressures towards strict observance had virtually disappeared, giving way to a day still different, if indefinably, from the rest of the week, but not having any clear character. 'The day thou gavest, Lord, is ended,' says a Sunday evening hymn, and that was about right, even by the nineteen thirties, though in a sense very different from the original sentiment.

Thus, to use the idea of the strait-laced Sundays of yesterday as an argument for accepting, without further ado, the loose-laced Sunday of today is not really valid. On the contrary, we are in a position, if we care to, to take a completely new look at the whole business, to examine it impartially, and to enquire whether there is not, after all, some gold hidden away at the heart of it. That there may well be is indicated by the fact that so many people for so many centuries thought highly of the Sabbath, and, later, of Sunday, and went to immense pains to preserve what they regarded as its sanctity. What were they getting at? What had they in mind? What happens, in short, when we blow some of the dust off this commandment and look with the unprejudiced eyes of people not having a Sabbatarian past to live down, upon what is to be found there?

The story is complex and extraordinary. It can be joined at almost any point, for the thread of the Sabbath runs through history like a river, and to follow that thread is the only way to arrive eventually at some understanding of what this commandment is saying to us now. When the Roman General Pompey, for instance, entered the Holy of Holies in the temple at Jerusalem in order to discover what the God of the Jews looked like, he knew, as did all the ancient world, that the Jews had another eccentricity besides the possession of an invisible God. They had also an inviolable Sabbath; the seventh day of the week which they observed with extreme strictness from sunset to sunset, and hedged around with regulations of fantastic detail. Thirty-nine classes of work were forbidden on the Sabbath, further sub-divided into thirty-nine subclasses, giving a total of well over a thousand actions which it was wrong to do on the sacred day, including sowing, ploughing, reaping, making a knot, untying a knot, putting out a fire. This is the background which makes sense of the trouble in which Jesus was involved when it was observed that his disciples, passing through the cornfields on the Sabbath, plucked ears of corn and rubbed them between their hands. They were reaping and threshing. Similarly, when Jesus himself made clay and laid it upon the eyes of the blind man he was guilty of a double breaking of the

Sabbath Laws in that the making of the clay meant work and the placing it upon the eyes meant healing.

This, the Sabbatarianism of Judaism, has a long reach into history. Victor Gollancz, recalling a Jewish childhood in his book, *My Dear Timothy*, records that, among other prohibitions of the Sabbath, no one was allowed to mend the fire or to strike a match or to smoke, because to do any of these things would have been to cross the magic line, drawn by ancient law, between the permitted and the forbidden.

[handwritten margin note: a would gas or Electric fire be allowed.]

Yet—and this is an odd thing—many in the ancient world regarded the strict Sabbath of the Jews not only with puzzlement, but also with profound admiration. Many old beliefs were on the way out: rather like our own, that world was a place of many uncertainties. And yet, right in the middle of them, was this rock-like religion of the Jews characterised, indeed made chiefly noteworthy by, this extraordinary institution of the Sabbath. Come what may, when the seventh day came round, the Jews would withdraw themselves until sunset brought release. It was a discipline; it was a mystery; it was something which gentile converts—and there was quite a number of them—found in their own experience to be most valuable. So there was another side to the matter apart from such absurdities as not being allowed to perform the smallest labour on the sacred day. And this mixture of absurdity on the one hand and of something of great value on the other, has persisted in the Sabbath story throughout the ages, and persists still.

But where did it all start? There is a clue here as to the relevance of this 'day off a week' principle to our city lives now. The commandment can scarcely have originated in the distant nomadic past of the Hebrew people. To down tools on one day of the week, for whatever reason, is not the kind of thing that would fit into the pattern of the wandering life of the desert. The demands of moving flocks could not possibly be adjusted to such a requirement. And what common sense suggests, history substantiates—that it was not until far later in their development, when much had happened to them, when they had known national disaster and exile, and when some had returned to the ancient land of their past, that the Sabbath as a characteristic institution of Judaism came into being. So it was the Jews of the cities, or at any rate of a settled life, who began to make much of Sabbath observance. This makes an interesting comment on much criticism in the modern world of the whole idea of setting aside one day of the week for rest, that it cannot be fitted into the pattern of things nowadays when so many of us live in an asphalt jungle and so few of us among the simplicities of nature. The history of the development of the Sabbath suggests, on the contrary, that it is just when people become committed to city life—as we have—that they need this weekly pause more than ever.

The Bible has two significantly differing versions of the origin of the Sabbath. The first occurs in Exodus: 'Six days shalt thou labour, and do all thy work: but the seventh day is a Sabbath unto the Lord thy God: in it thou shalt not do any work, thou, nor thy son, nor thy daughter, thy man-servant, nor thy maidservant, nor thy cattle, nor thy stranger that is within thy gates: for in six days the Lord made heaven and earth, the sea, and all that in them is, and rested the seventh day: wherefore the Lord blessed the seventh day, and hallowed it' (Exodus 20. 8-11).

The second is from Deuteronomy: 'Observe the Sabbath Day, to keep it holy, as the Lord thy God commanded thee. Six days shalt thou labour, and do all thy work: but the seventh day is the Sabbath unto the Lord thy God: in it thou shalt not do any work, thou, nor thy son, nor thy daughter, nor thy manservant, nor thy maidservant, nor thine ox, nor thine ass, nor any of thy cattle, nor thy stranger that is within thy gates; that thy manservant and thy maidservant may rest as well as thou' (Deuteronomy 5. 12-14).

The difference between these two accounts lies in the field of motive, in the reason given for observing the day. The first represents the Sabbath as an institution not made for man; but as something which man was expected to observe for reasons external to himself, in other words, as starting from something which God did rather than from something which man needs.

The second—it is, incidentally, much the older of the two—gives as the reason for the Sabbath that it shall be, for as many people as possible, an opportunity for rest. And when, for 'thy manservant and thy maidservant' we read, say, 'the bus driver, the waitress, and anybody else involved in working for us on Sundays,' we can at least begin to see what it is getting at. The main point, however, is just this: that the day is seen, in the second of these two accounts of its origin and purpose, as an institution based firmly on human need. The words of Christ, when he confronted the Sabbatarians, come immediately into the picture and point the way towards evaluation of this matter now: 'The Sabbath was made for man; not man for the Sabbath.'

There are obvious objections, for the modern mind, to the Exodus account, in any event. Literal interpretation of the creation story in Genesis has long ceased to be generally acceptable, and the idea of a God who was so wearied by his six days' labour that he needed rest and refreshment on the seventh presents, to say the least of it, a peculiar idea of deity. But these are details, easily enough explained by the antique framework of their origins. The main objection to thinking of the Sabbath in ecclesiastical rather than in sociological terms—which is exactly what the Exodus account of its origins is doing—is that it leads to Sabbatarianism, the insistence on, and imposition of, strict observance of the day whether we like it or not. An understanding of this curious and repulsive phenomenon, which has done more than anything else to devalue the original concept of the day as one of rest, refreshment, and uplift, is essential to any approach to the true meaning of the fourth commandment.

Sabbatarianism, then, has had an enormous history.

There is a direct line of descent from the kind of thinking which resulted in prohibitions of lighting a fire, or lifting an ox from a pit, or healing a man on the Sabbath, to all attempts in any age to regulate the observance of the day by legislation. Such attempts have led to some extraordinary results. As early as A.D. 600, Pope Gregory the Great felt moved to protest against advocates of Sabbatarianism who had made it illegal to have a bath on the sacred day. James I in 1618, and his son after him, both felt it necessary to moderate the Sabbatarian enthusiasms of their age by authorising *The Book of Sports* in which games and dances after church on Sundays were officially stated to be in order. In the late nineteenth century there had to be arguments before museums and even parks were opened. And even now some restrictions on Sunday trading and the like, some of them reflected in odd ways on the statute books, still exist, to the justifiable irritation of many. A *Report on the Law of Sunday Observance*, 1964, is the most recent look at the whole matter.

There are at least three very serious objections to Sabbatarianism. The first is that it is neither in temper nor in origin Christian; the second, that, being based on the principles of restriction, it does more harm than good; the third, that its basis rests on a wholly misleading demarcation between sacred and secular.

The first Christians were Jews, and so naturally ob-

served their Sabbath. But also they came to regard the
first day of the week, Sunday, with especial reverence
because it commemorated the day on which Christ rose
from the dead. Hence it was 'the Lord's Day,' and Christians met together for worship on that day from the earliest
days of the faith. But as Christianity grew outward into
the gentile world the Jewish Sabbath gave place to the
first day of the week. It never had the word 'holy' attached
to it, signifying 'set aside,' as did the Sabbath. It follows
that, in the earliest times, Sunday was seen by the Christians as a day for worship and for rejoicing but not as a day
for prohibition. And the non-Christian nature of the
Sabbath is emphasised by the fact that whereas the
observance of it is urged throughout the Old Testament
there is no such element in the New, either as regards the
Sabbath or even Sunday itself.

But by far the most unchristian element in Sabbatarianism is that by strictly demarcating one day from the rest
and calling it 'holy,' it implies that all the rest are in fact
unholy. People conditioned by this kind of thinking may
only too easily assume that it does not matter what is
done on the other six, provided that everything that is
'correct' is done on the seventh. This indeed has actually
come to pass more than once in human history. The great
point is that any division of life between what is sacred
and what is secular is fundamentally un-Christian because
it collides with the principle laid down by Christ that all
things are God's and are therefore all equally sacred.
Going to the office is sacred, so is going to bed with one's
wife; so is laughter, so are tears, so are joys and sorrows;
so in fact is the whole business of living. Thus, to set aside
a certain day of the week, and to say 'it belongs to God'
far more than the others is a serious denial of a vital truth.
Men have always tried to departmentalise religion, because
its claims could be made so much less troublesome when the

area of its operations was limited. As Studdert Kennedy put it in another context: 'Christ is perfectly harmless so long as he is kept shut up in churches. There is always trouble when you let him out.'

So it might be said that the Christian religion is perfectly harmless so long as its claims and disciplines can be confined to one day of the week; but that it becomes a much sterner affair when its claims are seen to be relevant to every day. We are in trouble as soon as we begin to think that holiness can be exclusively attached to or identified with any particular day. Paul in his letters quite often had to warn against this very attitude. He was writing to his Galatian converts with some irritation when he said: 'You keep special days. You make me fear that all the pains I spent on you may prove to be labour lost' (Galatians 4. 10). How can they be bothered with such arid matters, he has been asking them, once they have, as he had hoped, experienced the liberation from outdated compulsions which comes from the knowledge and experience of Christ? The question might be taken as the final verdict on Sabbatarianism in its more repellant aspects.

What then is left of this commandment which is meaningful for us today? A great deal; for the second of the two biblical accounts of the day's origin makes it quite plain that the 'day off a week' principle lay at the heart of the whole thing. This is a principle being progressively eaten away now. Sunday work is often prized, sometimes through necessity, because of the extra money it brings. And the whole shape of life now, its mobility, its long week-ends— soon almost certainly to be longer—has altered the whole framework of reference of this commandment. But none of this affects the root of the matter, which is that the most ancient and the most fundamental value of the Sabbath or of Sunday—call it what we will—lies in the principle of rest and refreshment, which every one of us needs, and always will.

What we do with the time of rest is up to the individual conscience. It is perfectly possible to get a restful Sunday by staying in bed. Whether it is possible to get a re-creative Sunday by doing so is another matter altogether. Anyone who cares to look impartially at the average Sunday as it has evolved now, and is prepared to clear his mind of prejudices inherited from a dead past, must surely ask himself whether we cannot do better things with the day than modern social patterns have brought about. It is not a moral judgement, but a sociological comment to say that the picture of the average winter Sunday, starting with the papers and ending with the telly, is a dreary one; and that the picture of the average summer Sunday on the roads is an increasingly crazy one. We ought, all of us, to be able to do better than that.

If it is right—and it is proved to be so by history and experience—that Sunday should be a day off, there are powerful arguments for the further principle that it should also be a day *on*; used for the re-creation of body and soul; used constructively in the highest sense. And the more it loses meaning, the more it becomes merged in the rest of the week, the further away, in fact, that this fourth commandment is allowed to drift out of the general consciousness, the less will this be possible. Is it really out of the question that on Sunday we should try to hear some serious music, read something of importance, look upon something that is fair, get our noses for a moment out of the admass pig-trough, and at least pause to wonder what life is all about? Maybe those earnest people who years ago used to fight, usually unsuccessfully, to get art galleries opened on Sunday, had something after all.

For practising Christians the picture is naturally much clearer. As inheritors of a tradition which sees Sunday as a commemoration of Christ's resurrection, as a time of seeking to meet with him again, the day has a ready-made special character of its own. Admittedly, to go to church on Sunday, and therefore to keep clear, as far as may be, from the pattern, both in thinking and doing, of the rest of the week, is nowadays by no means easy, and the less attractive church itself is—as many are—the harder it becomes. It is certainly far more difficult than in the days when there were, quite simply, less things to do, less attractive counter-demands on time and energy. But the duty, for the Christian who means business, is nonetheless there, of making church a part of Sunday, however much it means going against the tide of current patterns of social behaviour or personal inclination. Even so, there is nothing in this Christian tradition or in this fourth commandment to suggest that people should not enjoy themselves on Sundays. Anything to the contrary is a product of Sabbatarianism. A Sunday not enjoyed, in fact, is a Sunday wasted.

In the days when Christianity was a struggling sect—as it seems likely to become again—existing in the midst of a pagan world, the Romans came to suspect that Sunday was a day of nameless orgies, probably of a sexual nature, because Christians seemed to enjoy it so much. Yet when such an official as Pliny the younger, who, as governor of a province in the early years of the second century, had to examine Christians under oath, he found that the Sunday activities amounted to nothing more sensational than that of 'singing hymns to Christ as God, binding themselves together by solemn oaths to live honourable lives, and joining together in a common meal.' In other words, the day was made for them by its element of worship and meeting together.

Here, then, are the principles underlying the constructive use of Sunday. Here also, hidden away as usual, are the deepest meanings behind this fourth commandment. For here is a day which cannot be its real self unless it has in our own lives a different atmosphere and a different tempo from the rest. The observance, in the widest sense, of Sunday, is a part of the hygiene of living. We need, and need terribly badly, this regular pause from the tensions and pace of things, and we have never needed it more than we do now. Naturally, in a world which has gone so far the other way, as ours has by this time, some real personal discipline and conviction is required of anyone who tries along these lines to make anything of the day in terms of rest, and refreshment, and worship.

SOME QUESTIONS ABOUT THE FOURTH COMMANDMENT

1. Do you think it a good idea that Sunday should be, as far as possible, a day off from work?
2. Do you think Sunday ought to be anything else?
3. How do you find Sundays in general; enjoyable, uninteresting or no different from any other days?
4. Have you ever been bored by Sunday by being made to observe it too strictly?
5. Have you ever been bored by Sunday by not observing it at all?
6. Which do you think is worse?
7. What kind of Sunday, in your view, would be better than either?
8. 'A Sunday not enjoyed is a Sunday wasted.' Do you agree?
9. What do you think of the average modern Sunday?
10. How, if at all, would you improve it?
11. 'The Sabbath is made for man; not man for the Sabbath.' What do you think Christ meant by those words?

12. 'Remember the Sabbath day, to keep it holy.' What in practice does that mean for you?

SOME THOUGHTS ON THE FOURTH COMMANDMENT

Sabbath and Sunday

Albeit this (fourth) commandment of God doth not bind Christian people so straitly to observe the utter (external) ceremonies of the Sabbath day, as it was given to the Jews; as touching the forbearing of work and labour in time of great necessity, and as touching the precise keeping of the seventh day after the manner of the Jews; for we now keep the first day, which is the Sunday, and make that our Sabbath, that is our day of rest, in honour of our Saviour Christ, who as upon that day rose from death conquering the same most triumphantly; yet notwithstanding whatever is found in the commandment appertaining to the law of nature, as a thing most godly, most just, and most needful for the setting forth of God's glory, it ought to be retained and kept of all good Christian people.

The Book of Homilies: Homily on the Time and Prayer

The Christian Sunday

I was in the Spirit on the Lord's Day. *Revelation 1. 10.*

> *Bright shadows of true rest! some shoots of bliss;*
> *Heaven once a week;*
> *The next world's gladness prepossessed in this;*
> *A day to seek*
> *Eternity in time; the steps by which*
> *We climb above all ages; lamps that light*

78

Day off a Week

Man through his heap of dark days: and the rich
And full redemption of the whole week's flight.

Henry Vaughan: Sundays

On the 13th of the same month he [Johnson] wrote in his journal the following scheme of life for Sunday:

'Having lived' (as he with tenderness of conscience expresses himself), 'not without an habitual reverence for the Sabbath yet without that attention to its religious duties which Christianity requires:

1. To rise early, and in order to do it, to go to sleep early on Saturday.
2. To use some extraordinary devotion in the morning.
3. To examine the tenour of my life, and particularly the last week; and to mark my advances in religion, or recession from it.
4. To read the Scriptures methodically with such helps as are at hand.
5. To go to Church twice.
6. To read books of Divinity, either speculative or practical.
7. To instruct my family.
8. To wear off by meditation any worldly soil contracted in the week.'

Boswell's Life of Johnson, July 1755

He said, he would not have Sunday kept with rigid severity and gloom, but with a gravity and simplicity of behaviour.

ibid, September 1769

Sound Advice

It is better to plough upon holy days, than to do nothing, or to do viciously.

The Plain Man Looks at the Commandments

He that is choice of his time will also be choice of his company, and choice of his actions: lest the first engage him in vanity and loss; and the latter, by being criminal, be a throwing his time and himself away.

Jeremy Taylor: 1613-67

As the heavy is the foundation of the light, so is repose the foundation of action. *Taoist saying*

Learn to Relax

Rest and success are fellows. *Proverb*

He who sees how action may be rest and rest action: he is wisest among his kind; he has the truth. He does well— acting or resting. *Hindu saying*

A Testimonial

Sunday clears away the rust of the whole week.

Joseph Addison: 1672-1719

V Fathers and Mothers

Honour thy father and thy mother, that thy days may be long upon the land which the Lord thy God giveth thee.   *Exodus 20. 12*

The great question here is, quite simply, why? Respect for age and seniority, as such, for so long a built-in feature of family life, has been on the way out for some time. And, as with Sabbatarianism, there is a collective memory of a repressive past to be got rid of before the question of exactly why, if at all, parents should be 'honoured,' can be looked at impartially. There was a time when 'elders and betters' seemed to have all the plums in life: literature is rich in repressive fathers, demanding mothers, and children who were required to be seen and not heard. But now youth calls the tune; or at least does not have a tune called for it. Yet even in this new freedom, it is worth while, to say the least of it, to try and find what, if anything, this commandment has to say to us still.

It is always possible—and the possibility must be honestly faced—that it might not have anything to say, so completely have conditions changed. It is equally possible that what it has to say of value now, especially as regards *reasons* for honouring parents, turns out to be considerably different from what, for many centuries, it was understood as saying. To dig down to the foundations of the ideas underlying this commandment and to compare what is revealed with conditions as we know them is to get a startling glimpse of the degree to which the world has changed for us all.

It is quite clear, for instance, that fathers and mothers

in the fifth commandment are thought of as old; and the honouring of them as part of the mingled respect and compassion due to age. Now the whole principle of care and consideration for the old, like the principle of the maintenance of the family as a unit, with which it is involved, goes back to the very beginnings of civilisation and has been universally regarded as belonging to the category of natural duties. So the ungrateful or indifferent child has been regarded with abhorrence in many cultures. Among such people as the Jews, with their very strong tribal and family sense, the feeling was particularly strongly developed. 'Cursed be he that sitteth light by his father or mother,' is included in Deuteronomy in a list of maledictions along with other horrid deviations from normal conduct such as incest, indecency, and cruelty. And indeed parents generally were old by the time their children had grown up. For centuries to be fifty meant having at least one foot in the grave and to be over seventy suggested a toothless object of veneration. The whole picture changes dramatically, however, when a mother, still young at forty, can without difficulty take on a daughter of sixteen at tennis, or a father of fifty show himself every bit as tough as a son of twenty. Parents of this sort can be companions, if they choose; medical science and a greatly increased expectation of life have made it possible. But in such circumstances 'honouring' them, in the sense of revering their age, doesn't really make much sense.

And then again, a basis for this special attitude towards fathers and mothers lay in the fact that they were the repositories of special skills: they knew how to do things, and this knowledge they passed on to their young. If they did not do so, before the days of general education, no one else would, and the neglected or orphaned child grew up in ignorance. Thus, in the desert nomad life where this commandment was born, fathers would teach sons the know-how of flocks and herds, of defence and attack, and mothers would teach daughters the ways of women. In essentials, the same pattern continued for centuries: the farm labourer had a lot of know-how to pass on to his sons; so did the craftsmen, the wheelwrights, the smiths, the wood-cutters of those times long past; so did the farmer; and their wives had much to teach their daughters which nobody else could. Nor is this wholly vanished yet. There still remains detectable a special relationship between some farmers and their sons—even in these days of big-business agriculture—even between some men running one-man businesses, such as garages, and their sons. And this can generally be identified as the bond based upon the passing-on of know-how from one to the other. But the picture is different when the father works on an assembly line or, for that matter, behind a desk, and the mother likewise, as often happens. Such parents are not necessarily, or even at all, less kindly or well intentioned—they might even be a good deal more so than many of their heavy-handed predecessors. But their status as repositories of wisdom and passers-on of know-how has inevitably been greatly reduced. Some, indeed, have given up this teaching function of parenthood altogether, as can be seen, to give one example, in the cry that it is schools, not parents, who should be responsible for sex-education.

More and more, indeed, the state takes over areas of responsibility which once belonged to fathers and mothers. The extension of state functions into the fields of education, health and welfare—admirable and desirable as they all may be—has nevertheless, to some extent, taken away the responsibilities of the family.

So here again another traditional basis for the 'honouring' of fathers and mothers has been removed, or much reduced, by changing conditions.

And then again there is the matter of support. For centuries, children had to look to their parents for food and shelter. Fathers and mothers were the universal providers, and often enough the providing meant sacrifice. Obviously, up to a point this is still true: children still have to be fed and clothed. But it has for a long time been unnecessary for parents to pay anything towards a child's education or medical care unless they wish to. What is more, it is quite possible for sons and daughters actually to earn more than their parents within a few years of getting a job, sometimes because they have been better educated, sometimes because they have just been luckier. But, whatever the reason, the 'honouring' of parents as universal providers is no longer quite so easy.

But what about honouring them as givers of life? This is a deeper matter altogether. Is it a good thing to be born at all? The terrifying possibilities latent in world-wide population explosion at least make the question worth asking. 'Supposing that all the women in the world decide to procreate at their natural fertility rate, an Illinois professor has calculated that mankind will die of suffocation on 13 November 2026,' wrote Alfred Fabre-Luce in *Men or Insects*, a study of population problems. The statement may be an exaggeration, but the problem is real enough. With world population increasing at its present rate, social problems of the gravest sort, including even more widespread under-nourishment than at present is the case, will for very many inevitably become even more pressing. And anyone who contemplates the shape big-city life is assuming more and more, with its lacks of privacy, grace and quietude, cannot but be moved sometimes to wish there were less, not more people around, and to look forward with apprehension to a future when, according to the experts, they will have increased still further.

And yet to bring children into the world, and the more the better, has from earliest times been seen to be among the highest possible duties. More than a self-fulfilment for men and women, it has been regarded also as the discharging of a sacred trust, a passing on of the torch of life, a contribution towards ensuring the continuance of the race. All religions have blessed fecundity and deplored sterility. 'Children are an heritage of the Lord, and the fruit of the womb is his reward . . . happy is the man who has his quiver full of them,' says the 127th Psalm, reflecting an attitude which had altered very little over the years. The Church—especially the Roman Catholic Church— has encouraged the large family and frowned on means of preventing one, and many Communist states have taken the line that more meant better, and that parents of big families are therefore worthy of special honour, although some have now recognised the dangers of over-population. China, for one, has restarted contraceptive instruction and propaganda. In India, a land suffering gravely from over-population already, the almost universal prizing of parenthood as a status-symbol continues to present an intractable barrier to limitation of births. But mankind in general may well have to change these long-established ideas in the face of mounting pressures. The time may well come, in fact, when such things as family allowances will be paid to couples, not for having children; but for not having too many.

The whole basis of the fifth commandment is inevitably affected. If one of the strongest reasons for the honouring of fathers and mothers is that they are passers on of the torch of life, what becomes of this kind of thinking when it is generally recognised that parenthood is not necessarily a good or praiseworthy thing? Some drastic re-thinking is needed here. Meanwhile, almost all the traditional reasons for doing as this commandment says have to a considerable extent been swept away by changing conditions.

What then is left of the ancient building after this work of demolition? One thing is clear: a lot of fresh air has been let in, and some of the stuffiness which once afflicted the whole subject—such as the notion that children should somehow be grateful to parents for what was always the doubtful privilege of being brought into this world—has been let out. But foundations have been revealed as well. And it is there that there can be found bases for mutual honour and respect as between parent and child, far purer, less material, more loving and tender than anything envisaged in the commandment in older times.

Some little while ago, in a television programme concerned with old people, a significant exchange took place between the interviewer and an old lady living alone in a bed-sitting room. She was asked if she found life lonely. She said that she did. She was asked if she had any family. The reply was that she had two sons and one daughter, all married and with homes of their own. Lastly she was asked whether they visited her. And to that the answer was: 'They don't bother me, and I don't bother them.' It was perfectly plain and honest, and it was said without emotion. And yet, for reasons deeply embedded in the natures of most of us, for reasons, indeed, which derive from the whole shape of human society since the earliest times, there is something disquieting in such a narrative.

What are those reasons? Regard for parents is deeply embedded in human nature at its kindest and best. Nor is it merely a matter of having regard for them when they are old. As we have seen, age and parenthood do not go together as inevitably as once was the case. But the unease aroused, the sense of outrage engendered by indifference and neglect derives from a deeper source than the always rather shallow well of kindness. It derives from the ancient instinct to preserve the structure of the family—an instinct which itself springs from the even older one of self-preservation. When family life breaks up—and loyalty of its various members to each other is an essential part of it—society itself tends to break up. The strongest and happiest states have always been those in which family life and loyalties have been valued highly. This is the origin of reverence for ancestors and respect for the continuing traditions of clan and kind. Far back in time, when the ancestors of the people of the commandment lived the nomad life of the desert, they knew well that sticking together meant survival, that the straggler perished, and that unless families held together the tribe itself, the sum-total of them all, could have no future.

This is a truth having wide implications now. Any society which has disintegrated into a mass of individuals each seeking personal well-being has ceased to be a cohesive whole. And one aspect of such disintegration is the diminishing sense of love and respect for parents. The modern equivalent of what would have been seen, in the nomad life of the desert, as the ultimate enormity—the abandoning of an elderly parent—is remarkably like the state of affairs described by the old lady in the bed-sitter on TV. 'They don't bother me,' she said of her family. But there are profound reasons, of which a principal one is concern for the wholeness of the family, of the tribe or nation itself, why that is precisely what they should be doing. Admittedly, it was easier when families lived physically in closer contact than many do now. Re-housing of whole areas has, as a side effect, had damaging effects upon community sense. The fact that many people who have been re-housed in big cities like London or Birmingham, are often prepared to make long journeys back to the place they came from in order to get a drink in once familiar surroundings is a testimony to the strength of this kind of homing instinct. But if changing social conditions have made it more difficult to keep the com-

mandment 'honour thy father and thy mother,' they have
not made it less necessary: they have made it more so. We
are all in enough danger of falling apart at the seams as it is.
'No man is an island,' as John Donne said: our lives need
the framework of consciousness of ourselves as part of a
whole, as the son or daughter of someone; as part of a
family grouping. And that grouping becomes impossible as
soon as the loyalties underpinning it, of which respect for
parents is an integral part, are themselves undermined.

But there is a further reason for this 'honouring' of
parents. They are the providers of that all-important
factor in early life—environment. This is something which
has to be created. So parents in their capacity as home-
makers, and therefore as creators of the all-important
environment of the earlier years of life, are worthy of
respect, and deserving of love, in so far as they seek to
create an environment which gives to the child the best
as they see it. This is a high and solemn undertaking,
and the Bible is fond of drawing analogies between parent
and child and between God and man: 'Now, O Lord, thou
art our father: we are the clay, and thou our potter,' and so
on.

But the whole argument falls down, and the conditions
presupposed by the commandment are no longer present,
unless parents on their side are proving themselves up
to the job they have taken on. In other words, if fathers
and mothers are to be honoured, which means liked,
loved and respected, then they have to be worthy of it.
They are to be honoured because they are givers of protection and love, the age-old self-giving of fathers and
mothers since time began. Here is the deepest-seated and
most abiding reason of all why fathers and mothers—
always assuming that they are acting as such to the best of
their ability—are worthy of honour. For at the heart of
parenthood lies the principle of sacrifice. It is amply

reflected in nature. The nest-building birds, later devoting themselves with extraordinary application to feeding their young; and the sometimes fierce protectiveness of animals towards their offspring, all in their various ways show this principle in action. On the human side, it shows itself in an acceptance of responsibility for feeding, clothing, guiding and protecting children. No small job at any time, it can in some circumstances involve self-giving to the uttermost. This is the justification of love and respect for parents; this is the real reason for 'honour thy father and thy mother.' The motivation has to be one of gratitude, and it cannot be that unless parents themselves are measuring up to the tremendous responsibilities they have undertaken.

Every time we meet a sound, sensible and integrated man or woman, the kind of person we are glad to know, we are meeting the handiwork of their father and mother. And the opposite is true, as in the case of two charming small children who turned out badly, becoming anti-social, unhappy personalities incapable of coming to terms with their personal affairs whether marital, social, or financial. But they were not from a poor home; they were not from an unlucky home. They were just from a home where the parents' interest in them ended when they had been given food, clothing, and a bed. 'Honour thy father and they mother' was a nonsense here. There was nothing to honour, and the results were unfortunate. 'Children begin by loving their parents,' Oscar Wilde once said in a moment of truth. 'As they grow older they judge them; sometimes they forgive them.'

Successful parenthood is worthy of respect also because it is so difficult. Over-strictness can ruin it. So can over-slackness. So can over-possessiveness. Among the obstacles to happy marriage often mentioned by counsellors is the over-possessive parent on either side. And there is, too, the over-indulgent parent, who sees affection to be best expressed in giving to children what they want rather than in considering what, from time to time, might be good for them. And there is always to be encountered the over-ambitious parent who can make a child's life a misery by setting before it too high a level of attainment, especially educationally. Too often the failure of the child to 'keep up with the Joneses' in getting into what is considered the right kind of school is a source of deep unhappiness, and may with equal justice be classed as a condemnation of a certain kind of parent as well as of the educational system under which such things are possible.

Paul, as usual, touched the heart of the matter when he wrote to the Christians in Ephesus: 'Children, obey your parents, for it is right that you should. "Honour your father and mother" is the first Commandment with a promise attached, in the words: "that it may be well with you, and that you may live long in the land." You fathers, again, must not goad your children to resentment, but give them the instruction and correction which belong to a Christian upbringing.'

What is the meaning of those words 'that it may be well with you,' and 'that you may live long in the land'? This commandment, like all the others, was in the last resort addressed to the nation, as well as to the individuals in it. And hidden away here is once again the truth that upon the continuance and well-being of the family as a social unit, the very life of the nation must depend. Any which ignores the family in the end destroys itself because it is weakening that institution in which the best of human qualities—self-sacrifice, love in the deepest sense, and the recognition of the obligation of the stronger to the weaker, all have their natural place.

In the end it all comes down to a matter of loyalties and affection. Few, if any, are the materialistic reasons now left for the keeping of this commandment. But the spiritual or moral reasons are as strong, or even stronger, than ever. Whether parents can ever, need ever, or should ever, know they are being honoured is another matter. The final verdict on them may well belong not to their day at all but to some time in the years ahead when a child of theirs, maybe thumbing through some old photographs, will come upon a snap of a picnic, perhaps with a very ancient looking car in the background and two smiling people in the foreground. And he will pause, and lay his finger on them, and say: 'Those were my father and mother. They were good sorts.'

SOME QUESTIONS ABOUT THE FIFTH COMMANDMENT

1. What is your attitude to your parents? Love? Dislike? Indifference?
2. What are the most important things a parent has to offer a child today?
3. What is the relationship between parents and children in your family?
4. Are you satisfied with this relationship or could it be improved? If so, how?
5. Are there other older people that you honour more than your parents? Why?
6. Can you think of any sacrifices you have made consciously for your parents? And in what spirit were these sacrifices made?
7. Can you think of ways in which your parents have sacrificed themselves for you? Why do you think they did this?
8. In what way do you think modern conditions have altered the idea of respect for parents?
9. Do you think your parents made a good job of bringing you up?

10. How would you do the job differently?
11. Do you find you can 'honour' your parents? If so, why? If not, why?
12. What do you understand by 'that thy days may be long in the land which the Lord thy God giveth thee'?

SOME THOUGHTS ON THE FIFTH COMMANDMENT

The Duty of Parents

What man is there who, when his son asks for bread, will give him a stone?   *Matthew 7. 9*

The Duty of Parents to their children . . . is to be tender-hearted, pitiful, and gentle, complying with all the infirmities of children, and, in their several ages, proportioning to them several usages, according to their needs and their capacities . . . to secure their religion; season their younger years with prudent and pious principles; make them in love with virtue; and make them habitually so before they come to choose or to discern good from evil, that their choice may be with less difficulty and danger.

Jeremy Taylor: 1613-67

Train up a child in the way he should go: and even when he is old he will not depart from it.   *Proverbs 20. 20*

The Duties of Children

Children, obey your parents, for it is right that you should.   *Ephesians 6. 1*

Fathers and Mothers

A man should never hesitate to alleviate a father's or a mother's grief, even at the risk of his life.   *Buddhist saying*

A Word for Possessive Parents

It needs courage to let our children go, but we are trustees and stewards and have to hand them back to life—to God. As the old saying puts it: 'What I gave I have.' We have to love them and lose them.   *Alfred Torrie*

Private Lives

The joys of parents are secret; and so are their griefs and fears.   *Francis Bacon*

A Prayer for the Old

Lord, hear our prayer for those who, growing old,
Feel all their time of usefulness is told.
Let them still find some little part to play,
Nor feel unwanted at the close of day.

Anon

No Favourites

A parent should never make distinctions between his children.   *Talmud*

VI What Price Life?

Thou shalt do no murder.   *Exodus 20. 13*

Let's compare two things that are quite possibly taking place now; at this moment; as these words are read. The scene of the first is several hundred feet underground. It is very quiet down there: nothing, apart from equipment maintenance, ever happens; it is the devout hope of all concerned that nothing will. At a console an officer sits reading. What lights there are on the console—rather like the control desk in a television studio—are green; but there is a firing button marked with a light which could glow red. On the wall, adding to the studio atmosphere, is an electric clock with a large sweep of second-hand. Unseen and in darkness, tier after tier above, the cylindrical tube of the silo holds a missile, tipped by a war-head painted dull grey. Sealing off everything are doors, flush with the land around. But those doors can be slid open. And if they are, and if the man far below presses his button, the monstrous thing in the silo will rise, will soar from its hole in the ground, will settle into a long pre-determined trajectory aimed for a computer-calculated target. Within minutes, death on a stupendous scale will have been delivered to men and women thousands of miles away.

Very different is the other scene. Here also it is quiet; but there is a good deal more action. There is an operation in progress in one of the theatres of a great hospital. The patient is old: the complaint—it might be one of the many forms of cancer—is one for which fifty years ago there was no cure. But medical science has transformed the situation.

What Price Life?

Now, the theatre hums with a routine activity. Surgeon and staff, white-robed and masked, combine their skills with a rich variety of equipment to prolong a life which nature once would have taken. There is a little miracle in progress.

Pre-supposed and taken for granted behind both these scenes are two attitudes towards human life dramatically opposed. The man in the silo is at the terminus of a long assembly line of which the end product is death, to the achievement of which many marvellous skills have been brought, but which could not have begun at all without the basic assumption being made that, under certain circumstances, the infliction of mass-destruction is permissible. That no one wishes it to happen; that the missile and all the many other forms of the deterrent will have failed if it is ever used, does not alter the fact or the nature of the assumption. Similarly, the man and woman in the theatre are part of an assembly-line. Yet the end product of this one is life. Many skills have been brought to it, also, though the underlying assumption is that the preservation of life, the fanning of the tiny spark of it at any price and in almost any circumstances, is a first duty. The same people who thus prolong the existence of age would with equal zeal, and in accordance with the same honourable professional code, work to keep alive a helpless imbecile.

Here, in fact and as a fact, there stands a double standard towards human life which is relatively new. We might not be as overtly brutal as in the days of public executions; the road from hanging, drawing and quartering in public to the abolition of capital punishment is a long one, and has taken several centuries to traverse. But so is the road leading from the small-scale wars of the past to the indiscriminate mass-slaughter of today. Yet this one leads in the opposite direction; towards, rather than away from, brutality, and we have passed our own selves, as it were, travelling along each. While a new tenderness for life, especially towards the aged and sick, has been increasing on the one hand, warfare, to take one instance alone, has been becoming ever crueller. The first World War was far worse, as regards casualties, than anything known before. By the second, slaughter had come to include civilians as well as the military. On February 13th, 1945, when Allied bombers raided Dresden, 150,000 people died. Similar figures were reached with the first A-bomb drop on Hiroshima. Meanwhile, millions had died in Russia and in Hitler's concentration camps. And, in the years since, means of creating infinitely greater disasters have been developed. The conclusion is inescapable: that there has never, in the whole history of mankind, been a century so prodigal of the taking of human life as this.

It is easy enough to claim, of course, that it is not an increase of brutality but an increase of ingenuity which has made these things possible. But cities are not laid waste, nor do missiles lie in silos, unless a climate of opinion has somehow come to pass or, which is far more likely, a large-scale forgetting of ancient, grass-roots principles has taken place, which has removed moral issues from the arena and left only expediency behind. The great question is, therefore, whether there exist any ancient, grass-roots principles which still apply in so baffling and sinister a situation.

But it is essential not to over-simplify. Indeed, it is so important, and the rewards of getting at some of the real truth of the matter are so considerable, that it is worth-while spending a little time clearing out of the way some mis-apprehensions. That this commandment stands now, or was ever intended to stand as a total prohibition of the taking of life in any circumstances is simply not true. A look at its origins makes that plain enough.

It was born in a primitive society where the limitation

of killing was a necessity if any kind of civilised life was to be achieved. And what it prohibited was private killing for gain or vengeance. Judicial taking of life, or the slaying of the nation's enemies in time of war, were not covered by it, and it would have astonished any Jew of Old Testament times to find anyone supposing that they were. Indeed, he himself belonged to a martial and blood-thirsty race.

The Hebrews were warrior peoples. When they went to war, which they frequently did, they were concerned not so much with the basic ethics of their action as with the question of whether God was on their side. If he was, then all would be well. If he was not, then all would inevitably be lost. The concept of a 'just war' might perhaps be said to be peeping out of all this. But the concept of no war at all was certainly unknown.

The commandment is really concerned with the hard and unpalatable truth that man has always had the curse of blood upon him, and still has; that the taking of life, when it suits his convenience, has always come fearfully easy to him, as it still does. In the ancient world it needed only the flash of a dagger and the deed was done. In the modern world it needs only the pressing of a button and again the deed is done. This is where the whole thing begins to link up with our own situation now, for the primary purpose of the commandment is to bring some order and principle into a situation where the taking of life, so easy to effect and so productive of dark satisfaction in the human psyche, needs to be checked and regulated by the highest possible moral sanction. The old 'eye for eye, tooth for tooth' idea was not so much a blood-thirsty ordinance as the very opposite —an attempt to limit the scope of inter-tribal vengeance. It was not nearly so senselessly cruel as the bombing of Dresden or as appalling and indiscriminate in its killing as would be the letting of that missile out of its silo.

So therefore this sixth commandment represents an

attempt to impose some kind of restraint upon the killing instinct in man, and to implant in his mind a due sense of the solemnity of taking a human life in any circumstances, even though that taking may have been held at times to be necessary.

Nor is it accurate to claim to find in this commandment an argument against capital punishment. The framers of it would have been as astonished by that conclusion as by the view that it condemned war in any form and in any cause. Indeed, it is an ironical fact that it has quite often been used as a warrant *for* capital punishment, it being held that the breaking of so solemn a prohibition could be adequately punished only by the supreme penalty. Murder has been for centuries punishable by death not because life was held cheaply, but because it was in law prized very highly. The gallows have now virtually disappeared from the scene in most countries. But that disappearance has owed little, one way or the other, to the sixth commandment.

It is easy to become impatient here. If this commandment has nothing to say to us on these crucial issues of our day, what is the purpose of dwelling upon it? But it has something to say to us; something of vast import, which lies not superficially on the surface, but at depth. And the first truth it holds is that human life is sacred. We need to ask both what that means and why it should be so. The meaning is clear; that which is sacred is set apart, sacrosanct, because of an association with something larger than itself. So human life is made sacred—to those holding the high, deistic concept of human nature—by the fact of an association with its creator well expressed in the old words, 'In the image of God made he man.' The real importance of the words is the principle they lay down; that human nature, partaking in some respects of the divine, belongs ultimately to God. That fact alone makes of any taking of

98

human life at best an act of dreadful responsibility, and, at the worst, a sacrilege. The concept of the sanctity of human life is thus tied up with the parallel concept of the intrinsic worth of that life itself. 'Thou hast made him a little lower than the angels, and hast crowned him with glory and honour,' wrote a psalmist. The words have an antique ring. But they nonetheless enshrine a principle of enormous importance—that the individual human life is of immeasurable value in the sight of God. This truth took a long time to emerge from a past when men killed each other easily. It could disappear altogether in an age like the present when they can do it more easily still, by remote control, and without even getting their hands bloodstained.

So 'thou shalt do no murder,' is based on the truth of the uniqueness of human personality. Once that uniqueness has been lost sight of, a horrible incertitude creeps into human affairs. The gas chambers of Auschwitz and Buchenwald become possible. So does discussion about the possibility of multi-megaton death. The situation in which all of us find ourselves nowadays, of holding on, by a few precarious toeholds, to the slippery slope above the abyss, has not been created so much by the possession of mass means of destruction, as by the creation of a climate of opinion in which the use of them can be visualised. The ancient, grass-roots principle which the commandment enshrines becomes poignantly relevant at precisely this point—the principle of *reverence for life*. That is about all we have left, to shield us from the terrors of our own creation—this starkly simple conviction that every single individual life has a sacred significance. And this principle cannot be upheld on the foundations of sand which are all that sentiment or a vague humanitarianism can provide. It has to stand—indeed can only stand—on the rock of the conviction that man is a creature of God.

But regard for the principle of reverence for life involves also a concern for quality of life. Forgetfulness of this truth can lead to some very odd consequences indeed. If for instance, as seems highly probable, over-population degrades the conditions under which people live to the point of affecting their dignity and development as individual personalities, then a true reverence for life may well come to include a limitation of it. This same factor of over-population came into the picture in relation to the fifth commandment. Now here it is again, highly relevant to the sixth as well, which is an indication of how increasingly intrusive this formidable new element in human affairs is likely to be. Reverence for life and an unthinking proliferation of it to the point where dignified living becomes impossible must at some stage collide, and we might well be very near that stage now. In the east the point was reached and passed a long time ago.

The same consideration or reverence for the quality as well as the quantity of life is also raised by the unthinking prolongation of it. The surgeons and nurses in the theatre where the operation was being carried out upon an elderly patient—that scene which made such a contrast with the death-dealing missile in its silo—would have no doubt but that they were doing the right thing. Yet is this always the case?

For the Christian at any rate, another element in the situation has to be considered. The prolongation of human life for its own sake and at any price has never been seen, in Christian thinking, as an ultimate good. The sixth commandment prohibits the taking of life for selfish ends; it certainly does not advocate the prolonging of life for its own sake. It is not the fact that the heart keeps beating and the blood circulating which makes life precious, but the quality of the life livable. And quite often the extreme old age to which many—especially women—are today unwittingly condemned by medical care is more a burden than a blessing. Such is the hard truth behind the oft-discussed 'problem of the old' and what to do with them. We have to be careful, therefore, in trying to get at the relevance of this commandment now, to distinguish between a Christian unwillingness selfishly to take the life of another, and a readiness to see in the prolongation of life the ultimate good, merely because we have ceased to believe in anything after it.

What has brought about the extraordinary double-think in the modern world which makes it possible to be so unthinkingly tender of life on the one hand and to contemplate colossal, push-button murder on the other? The answer lies, surely, in the fact of our having lost touch with this ancient principle of reverence for life in its fullest sense— a reverence based upon an ingrained feeling that, since it belongs to God, it is not something for man to take away or unduly to manipulate or interfere with.

But undoubtedly the most sensitive point at which this commandment touches all of us now, is in relationship to the whole matter of our world's latest, most terrible bite from the apple of the tree of knowledge—the newly-acquired capacity of man to destroy himself. The missile in the silo, not the scene in the operating theatre, is that which burns most in the mind. After all, why should man not destroy himself?

Without an ear for the voice which spoke from Sinai, warning against the sin, always old and ever new, of murder, modern man need not be surprised if it comes upon him in many guises. The latest is this nuclear weapon. Logically, this surely represents the end of the road, as regards how far man can go on living without finally mastering his terrible and terrifying tolerance of murder in certain circumstances, such as the defence of 'a way of life' which he prizes. It is possible to argue for the possession of nuclear weapons on the grounds that they deter, and so make war less likely. But even this famous argument pre-supposes a willingness to use them, for without such a pre-supposition the so-called deterrent is a harmless and useless piece of bluff. But this sixth commandment is not concerned with questions of expediency, but solely with the rightness or wrongness of the taking of human life. Such taking of life has in the past been condoned under this commandment where it has been held to be fulfilling a higher purpose, such as upholding the cause of justice or defending the state against external enemies. But it is exceedingly difficult to see how such a commandment, having reverence for life at the heart of it, could possibly be held to condone the use of nuclear weapons, with their extraordinary and appalling capacities for impersonal and wholesale killing. Here is a new situation we all have to face, and it is becoming increasingly clear that we cannot adequately do so by using arguments from the past. But the sixth commandment does not present an argument from the past. It presents a principle of reverence for life as the creation and the property of God. It may well be, therefore, that as regards the use of nuclear weapons the time has come when 'unless we make up our mind in advance what we are not prepared to tolerate, unless we commit ourselves publicly to limits which we will not pass, experience in recent history should surely remind us that we are likely to find that no limits in fact exist which we are not prepared to transgress.'[1]

Of course, the only way off this slippery slope where decay of belief, increase in the means of destruction, lack of reverence for life and fear for our own skins has landed us, is by the more excellent way of Christ. We shall always have enemies. What he is telling us is to love them. We shall always have a propensity to murder. What he is telling

D M.MaKinnon: 'Ethical Problems of Nuclear Warfare' in *God*, *Seca d.*[1]*x anr*. Fontana Books.*W* us is to root out the mental attitudes which make it possible. 'You have learned that our forefathers were told, "do not commit murder: anyone who commits murder must be brought to judgement." But what I tell you is this: anyone who nurses anger against his brother must be brought to judgement.' We shall always have an urge to hang on to life at any price without consideration of the value of the life thus hoarded. But what he goes on saying to us is: 'Whoever cares for his own safety is lost; but if a man will let himself be lost for my sake, that man is safe.' Situated as we are now, failure somehow, sometime, to reach this standard might well be the end of us. Meanwhile, we still have that toe-hold above the abyss, and that toe-hold is the reverence for life which is the true meaning behind this sixth commandment.

SOME QUESTIONS ABOUT THE SIXTH COMMANDMENT

1. Do you think it right to prolong life in all circumstances, such as extreme age or incurable illness? If so, why?
2. Do you think it wrong to take life in any circumstances? If so, why?
3. We are making nuclear weapons. We are also more sensitive about preserving life than we used to be. Do you find anything odd in this? If so, what?
4. Do you think this commandment could be used to support the arguments against war in any form, conventional or nuclear? If so, how?
5. Can you agree with the view that human life is sacred?
6. What reasons would you give for saying that it was sacred?
7. What are your views on capital punishment?

8. Do you consider this commandment could be used in support of the case against capital punishment?

9. 'In the image of God made he man.' In what ways should acceptance of this view of human nature affect our attitude to human life?

10. What do you understand by the expression 'reverence for life'?

11. Would you want to prolong your own at any price?

12. 'Whoso careth for his own safety is lost.' What do you think Christ meant by those words?

SOME THOUGHTS ON THE SIXTH COMMANDMENT

Doctor's Prescription

> *Thou shalt not kill; but need'st not strive*
> *Officiously to keep alive.*
> > *A. H. Clough: The Latest Decalogue*

Human Life Sacred?

Experience had shown that the preparation of prussic acid called Cyclon B caused death with far greater speed and certainty, especially if the rooms were kept dry and gas-tight and closely packed with people, and provided they were fitted with as large a number of intake vents as possible. So far as Auschwitz is concerned, I have never known or heard of a single person being found alive when the gas chambers were opened half an hour after the gas had been inducted.

> *Rudolf Hoess: Commandant of Auschwitz*

What Price Life?

People were transfixed with fright at the power of the explosion. Oppenheimer was clinging to one of the uprights in the control room. A passage from the *Bhagavadgita*, the sacred epic of the Hindus, flashed into his mind.

> *If the radiance of a thousand suns*
> *were to burst into the sky,*
> *that would be like*
> *the splendour of the Mighty One—.*

Yet, when the sinister and gigantic cloud rose up in the far distance over Point Zero, he was reminded of another line from the same source:

> *I am become Death, the shatterer of worlds.*

Explosion of the first experimental atom bomb, 13 July 1945, from Robert Jungk's Brighter Than a Thousand Suns.

Weapons of war are tools of evil; those who truly admire them are murderers at heart.   *Taoist saying*

Concept of the Just War—Past

For a war to be just, three conditions are necessary: public authority, just cause, right motive. . . . Augustine declares that the decision and authority of declaring war lies with rulers, if the moral order is to be peacefully composed. . . . Those who are attacked should deserve to be attacked. . . . Those who go to war should fight to achieve some good or avoid some evil.   *St. Thomas Aquinas*

Concept of the Just War—Present

It is impossible to reject wholesale the doctrine of a just war, since it contains an important element of truth, that might become relevant even today in particular limited situations, where a non-atomic conflict was concerned. . . . But . . . the change brought about by the new weapons is that a war involving their use is no longer feasible as a means of defence. It inevitably destroys what it is supposed to defend. It is sheer nonsense to attempt to justify nuclear weapons and nuclear warfare on the basis of the traditional evaluation of arms and military protection and to deny the novelty of the problem presented by this technical development in warfare.   *Professor Helmut Gottwitzer*

VII The Great Sex Question

Thou shalt not commit adultery.   *Exodus 20. 14*

'The sooner it is recognised that the Church cannot stop non-Christian teenagers having sex together, the better.' That, from a national daily not long ago, is worth quoting mainly for three implications behind it: that there is a difference between Christian and non-Christian standards in these matters; that it is the exercise of a legitimate freedom for teenagers—or anyone else—to 'have sex' together if they feel like it; and that some person or persons unknown, collectively labelled 'the Church,' are trying to stop them. Which, if any, of these implications are true is an interesting question. Maybe the answer will emerge in the course of this. Meanwhile, one thing is clear, that opposition to sexual freedom is thought by many to be symbolised, summed-up, and framed in a characteristically heavy-handed manner by the seventh commandment: 'Thou shalt not commit adultery.'

Yet, strictly speaking, this commandment is not about fornication, which means sexual intercourse between the unmarried; or about chastity; but about adultery, which means a breach, by either husband or wife, of their marriage vows of faithfulness. But in life, which is notoriously a confused and muddled affair, all these things do in fact tend to get mixed together—fornication, adultery, casual sexual contacts, from the affair to the mutual exchange of favours after a dance, on a level well described in a lyric from the musical *What Makes Sammy Run?*:

The Plain Man Looks at the Commandments

Drinks are okay, they break the ice,
Dancing this way is also nice.
But why delay the friendliest thing two people can do?

Why indeed? That is the point. The real questions before us all nowadays are whether there can be—or should be—any longer any absolute standards in sexual conduct and, if so, what they are. Is chastity, for instance, still a valid or a praiseworthy ideal? Is it possible that the equation of virginity with virtue represents a psychologically unhealthy attitude towards sex itself—a reflection of the ancient 'flesh is evil' frame of mind? Can the concept of marriage as a sacred, indissoluble bond carrying with it the obligation of total sexual faithfulness any longer stand up to dramatically changed conditions; the independence of women, do it yourself contraception, increased expectation of life, so that often now a marriage has to endure longer than was once the case? There is certainly a gap between the generations in this field. 'Nothing,' wrote a young married woman to the *Daily Telegraph* recently, 'brings into clearer relief the division of the two generations than the question of sexual morality. It is my experience that the gulf is so wide that there is scarcely a point at which contact can be made between them. We look round the world our parents have created . . . and we feel they have little reason to preach at us. Their lives seem to have been based on "thou shalt not," and especially on the rule "thou shalt not be found out" . . . Instead of empty rules we would substitute love and understanding.'

Such obviously sincere views deserve respect. They certainly call for more thoughtful treatment than that of putting them up merely in order to knock them down again with the intention, or at least the hope, of proving in the process that the 'old ways' are best. That is impossible, in any event. There can be no going back to a morality based negatively on prohibition. The great

108

sexual revolution of our time has long passed the point of no return. 'Sex,' wrote a contributor to *Encounter*, 'to a surprising number of adolescents, is old hat; sexual freedom is casual and secondary—no longer a symbol of revolt. Many teenagers are a little shocked at their senior's pre-occupations with the subject. Others, constitutionally in-capable of being shocked, are exasperated by the im-portance adults seem to accord to an activity which the teenagers take as a matter of routine, almost as a matter of hygiene. . . . Freud broke the Tables of Chalk on which the Victorian moral code was engraved. Now it is quite possible, *pace* the professional moralists, to live wisely without a moral system. . . .'

It may be quite possible. But what is disagreeable is to live in a state of confusion about the whole thing, which in fact is precisely the condition of many of us now. And very often the confusion is the greater in proportion as people—and especially young ones—care, and genuinely want to know whatever answers there are to be had. There is only one kind of person who has no problem in fact: he who has no morals at all. For the rest, the going is tough. So if this seventh commandment really has anything still valid to say about sex relationships in general, there is importance in discovering what it is.

But, as with some of the other commandments, its true significance has to be dug for. And this dig has to begin on the surface, where certain obvious facts about the com-mandment's origin are to be found, and need to be noted. One very plain one is that it began in a man-dominated world, and was concerned not so much with 'purity' as with property—a husband's 'rights' to his wife.

Marriage itself began as a form of possession. A man took a woman perhaps by knocking her on the head. She remained his so long as he could prevent other men from knocking him on the head and carrying her off. Later on, as brute man crept slowly towards some kind of civilisation, he learned to conduct his affairs with less violence and a little more order, so that the long age arrived of marriage by purchase. A wife was bought, the purchaser paying an actual price in cash or goods. There are elements in the marriage service today which represent hangovers from this state of affairs. 'Who giveth this woman to be married to this man?' is a question which still represents her as a piece of property being handed over from one party to another. So the seventh commandment faithfully reflected this mercantile view of women. It was not in the least concerned with how a man thought of his wife and certainly not whether he 'loved' her. It was not concerned with his relationship with other women, provided they were un-married. What is more, the man could in law get rid of his wife; but not she of him. Right down to the time of Christ it was a matter for debate among Jewish schools of thought as to whether a husband could divorce a wife at any time and for any reason, or for no reason at all, or whether his only grounds for divorce should be sexual misconduct on her part. The question of his own conduct never entered into the picture.

This was the beginning of the two standards, the one for men and the other for women, which persisted until comparatively recently. Nonetheless, right at the heart of the commandment was certainly a high view of the importance of family life, and of the need to keep it inviolate, for the sake of the well-being of the nation as a whole.

Yet, if that were all that this commandment stood for, it could not be expected to have much to say to us now. The fact that it has is due to the deepening and widening of meaning which Christ gave it. With him, what was negative becomes positive; what started as a prohibition of one kind of sexual misconduct on the part of the wife becomes also a challenge to all concerned to clean up their minds and so make less likely modes of conduct which devalue the whole concept of sexuality. 'You have learned that they were told, "do not commit adultery," but what I tell you is this: if a man looks upon a woman with a lustful eye, he has already committed adultery with her in his heart.' So what began as a piece of legislation designed to protect the man's rights to his wife as a piece of property, became associated with a relationship between man and wife of a wholly deeper kind, in which mental attitudes loom as large as physical acts. Here was a teacher who said that marriage was for keeps, who perceived that the sexual act involved infinitely more than a coupling of bodies, but was ideally a mutual self-giving, based on a desire to share each other, and on an intermingling of personalities to a rare degree—that 'becoming one flesh' of which St. Paul later wrote. The deepening and widening which Christ gave to the original, comparatively simple prohibition of adultery lay therefore chiefly in up-grading the concept of the relationship which it was designed to protect.

Thus it came about that a commandment which originally stood guard over marriage as a business deal, came to be seen as something relating to marriage as a total relationship between man and woman. It follows that the relevance or otherwise of this commandment now is bound up with the question of whether the concepts which it seeks to protect—marriage as more than a legal compact, and chastity outside marriage on the grounds that sexual union itself involves total commitment—are any longer valid. And also bound up with it is the whole question of whether sexual 'freedom' as understood and now widely practised—sexual experience unfettered by moral inhibitions—can be maintained without a debasing of the whole currency of human relationships.

This is the place to take a look at the modern sexual revolution with which the answers to so many of these questions are bound up. But this revolution, like a coin, has two sides. The one bears the dignified markings of many efforts to find a new way with sex for a new age; the other carries the squalid marks of the almost manic sex-obsession which has become such a feature of our times. And both need to be looked at if any wholeness of view is to be obtained.

When we start with the first, with those honest efforts to find, as the young wife who wrote to the *Daily Telegraph* put it, 'instead of empty rules, love and understanding,' we are immediately in distinguished company.

Thus Professor Carstairs in his Reith Lectures: 'Contraception is still regarded as something wicked, threatening to chastity, opening the way to unbridled licence. But *is* chastity the supreme moral Virtue? In our religious traditions the essence of morality has sometimes appeared to consist of sexual restraint. . . .' And *Encounter*, in an article already quoted, had this: 'Genuine attempts are made from time to time to present the objective facts about sex on these islands rather than to save appearances. The Wolfenden Report is one outstanding instance, and the recent Report of the Society of Friends another. . . . The Quaker Report is, in fact, a remarkably clear-sighted and courageous document, as may be gathered from its final paragraph dealing with pre-marital sex experience, "which," says the report, "is not such a sin. Where there is genuine tenderness and openness to responsibility and the seed of commitment, God is surely not shut out".' Such instances of radical re-thinking of sexual attitudes—and they could easily be multiplied—have one thing in common—a calling in question of the whole principle of prohibition in this field, and a desire to replace it by love, in the highest sense of the word.

That expression 'love,' requires definition. It has always been a difficulty in English that one word has to carry the weight of several meanings. There is, for instance, the total misuse of it to betoken what is really the basic sex urge which, purely biological in origin, requires for fulfilment only a coupling of bodies, for which any woman or any man will suffice. We can call this Venus. Then there is what the Greeks called Eros, which is fundamentally a need to fill up what is sensed as a gap in life, a need for completeness, a need which can find various forms of satisfaction but which has often expressed itself best in romantic love, the force behind the chance sniping of Cupid on top of a bus, whereby boy and girl each makes the marvellous discovery that, for a time at any rate, the other is the only boy (or girl) in the world. Eros can be a very fine thing, a generous emotion; but as a sex relationship it is highly idealised and carries within it the seeds of its own dissolution. The snag in being Romeos and Juliets is that no one can keep to that level all the time. Eventually they have to begin living together as persons, having breakfast together, growing older together. In that process a third kind of love, Agape, self-giving, asking nothing, plays an essential part.

Trouble arises when all these utterly different kinds of 'love' get mixed up. Above all confusion comes when the whole lot become equated with 'sex' as in 'the sooner it is recognised that the Church cannot stop non-Christian teen-agers having sex together, the better.'

And this confusion has actually happened, and can be seen on a very large scale in that obsession which is the reverse side of the sexual revolution of our times. It is not necessary to be reactionary to feel angrily sad at this sickness which shows itself in so many ways: from the cult of the so-called 'daring,' through the constant harping on sexual themes in kitchen-sink drama, to the spectator sex of the pornographic magazines with their endlessly repetitive pictures of female flesh. None of this has anything to do with Eros or Agape, only with Venus, and represents a debasing of our common sexuality which all men and women of goodwill may well deplore. And the fact that it is based on nothing more complicated than that sex is a strong selling line for all manner of goods, services and entertainments should not be allowed either to obscure or to excuse the immense social harm of it all. 'It remains for each man and woman to walk through the sexual bombardment and determine for themselves what to them seems tasteless or objectionable, entertaining or merely dull. . . . But no one can really calculate the effect this exposure is having on individual lives and minds.' It is not easy to disagree with that, from a splendid article in *Time* not so long ago. Like bacteria in drinking water the 'provocative' is socially poisonous, especially as it pulls down to the level of the monkey-house questions of sexual behaviour which deserve all the intelligent treatment they can get. It has never been easy to live responsibly with sex in a civilised society. It becomes more difficult than ever when commercialised sex finds good business in stoking fires without caring what they consume.

One way of treating such a confused situation of which this kind of thing is an example—the exploitation of the idea of restraints by representing it as daring to defy them —is by removing the restraints altogether. As strip-tease would be meaningless in a society which practised nudity, so would promiscuity cease to be alluring, and the denial of it thought to be injuriously repressive, as soon as it was taken as a matter of course. In other words, on this theory, take sex out of the realm of morals altogether, like taking the fangs out of a cobra, and it becomes possible to live happily ever after with the creature.

Quite clearly there is some truth in this. Since Freud, we

have come to know more of the psychological perils of sexual repression. But it becomes increasingly clear that permissiveness as well as repression has its dangers and can have its tragedies. People can be 'hurt in their sex,' to use a phrase of Laurence Durrell's, by other things than by having to go without it, or by being made to feel guilty about it. The disappointing rise, after many years' decline, in the incidence of venereal disease, in spite of antibiotics, is a sombre fact. So is the far more startling rise in illegitimacy rates, notably among young people, a wry commentary upon an age which professes to know so much about sex and its techniques.

Such things are sad indeed. But scant service is done to anybody by using them as an argument for a return to a so-called stricter moral code. The past made a mess of its sex, in some respects, as well, and the record of repression is not a very attractive one. What is much more important, among the by-products of sexual permissiveness, is the loss of that very precious thing, a high, dignified, even beautiful concept of the sex-relationship as the ultimate expression of the total love—combining Venus, Eros and Agape: passion, need, and self-giving—of a man and woman for each other. The point here is that such a valuation cannot co-exist with a view of sexual activity as an aspect of personal hygiene or even as just 'the friendliest thing two people can do.' We can't have it both ways because this high ideal of total love, involving sexual activity as one among its many elements, carries with it the implication of uniqueness. It is something for one man and one woman, something peculiar to just the two of them, a relationship they have created between themselves, something which cannot be repeated with all and sundry.

Sex can always be devalued by making it easy; just as diamonds could be devalued by flooding the market with them. But both in the process cease to be precious. The

Victorians, it has been well said, talked a lot about love, yet knew little about sex. It could be that we, who talk much about sex, could think a bit more about love.

'You have learned that they were told "do not commit adultery"; but what I tell you is this: if a man looks upon a woman with a lustful eye, he had already committed adultery with her in his heart.' The words become very relevant at this point, bringing into the whole picture of sex-relationships today the commandment as Christ broadened it. Much of what goes for 'sex' now is in fact and fundamentally just this, 'looking upon woman with a lustful eye.' As a mental attitude, it is damaging to a total relationship based upon love. And furthermore, since marriage upon a basis of permanence, life-sharing, and loyalty is the only human relationship so far invented which can provide the foundation for the exercise of total love between man and woman—a relationship which is always imperilled by adultery—the commandment proclaims a standard as meaningful today as ever it was.

Yet marriage continues to be an essential institution. No society with any semblance of a claim to a civilised ordering of its affairs has ever been able to manage without it. It is by coming together, by the fusion of personality in this total relationship that a man and woman can become 'one flesh,' and make sense out of what can so very easily become the non-sense of sexual activity divorced from love and loyalty.

What is involved is the whole matter of our sexual code of behaviour. It is quite possible that we are ceasing to have one, or at any rate replacing the prohibitions of the past with a greater permissiveness which some would hail as a new triumph for the liberal spirit. Meanwhile, while the matter is being argued, and while many people— especially young ones—continue to find it difficult to come upon any standards sufficiently compelling to compete with the counter-attractions of earlier physical maturity and constant sexual suggestiveness, it is not a bad idea to revalue such standards as we have. Of these, Christian marriage is certainly one. And of that institution this commandment has been for long ages seen as one of the sentinels.

SOME QUESTIONS ABOUT THE SEVENTH COMMANDMENT

1. What does the word 'sex' mean to you?
2. Do you agree that there is a marked division between the attitude of older and younger people nowadays towards sexual relationships?
3. Can you think of any reasons for this division?
4. How important would you rate chastity?
5. How important would you rate the idea of marriage for keeps?
6. Do you see any connection between the two?
7. How do you feel about promiscuity, not in theory but in practice? Would it bother you whether your fiancée or wife, boy friend or husband, slept around with others?
8. If so, why?
9. What do you understand by the term 'love'?
10. Can you think of any ways in which it is currently abused?
11. How would you regard the 'spectator sex' of the girlie magazines: as fun, a bore, or an evil?
12. 'The Victorians talked a lot about love, yet knew little about sex. It could be that we, who talk much about sex, could do to think a bit more about love.' Do you agree?

The Plain Man Looks at the Commandments

Three Kinds of Love

There are three kinds of love; false, natural and married. False love is that which seeks its own, just as one loves gold, goods, honour or women outside of matrimony contrary to God's command. Natural love is between father and children, brother and sister. But above them all is married love. It burns as fire, and seeks nothing more than the mate. It says, 'I wish not yours; I wish neither gold nor silver, neither this nor that. I want only you.'   *Martin Luther*

One Kind of Marriage

'Ah, dear God, marriage is not a thing of nature but a gift of God: the sweetest, the dearest, and the purest life above all celibacy and all singleness, when it turns out well, though the very devil if it does not.'   *Martin Luther*

Marriage for Keeps

The greater the friendship the more permanent it should be. The greatest friendship is that between man and wife, who are coupled not only by physical intercourse, which even among animals conduces to a certain sweet friendship, but also for the sharing of domestic life.

St. Thomas Aquinas

The Great Sex Question

The Root of all Virtue

Lust and pride are the roots and sprouts of vice, as the desire for happiness is the root of all virtue.

St. Thomas Aquinas

A Reminder

At a time when a large part of mankind is beginning to discard Christianity, it is worth while to understand clearly why it was originally accepted. It was accepted in order to escape at last from the brutality of antiquity. As soon as we discard it, licentiousness returns, as is impressively exemplified by life in our modern cities.

C. Jung

Taking Our Pleasures Sadly

In the earlier periods of sexual obsession a lot of its force lay just in the fact that sexual enjoyment is fun, and gains a zest from the prohibitions of its indiscriminate exercise by a tradition of customs and morals. Departures from the tradition were dashing, daring and naughty escapades. Now, this is no longer so. Venereal experiences outside marriage are either casual, or invested with a solemn prophylactic significance, on the grounds that suppression produces mental disease.

V. A. Demant: Christian Sex Ethics

The Plain Man Looks at the Commandments

A More Excellent Way

The practice of Christian sex ethics is not to be recovered by preaching the ethics. . . . A renewed, creative and fully personal fulfilment of sexuality will only come from people who are aware of the pressure of a debilitated civilisation and, without contracting out of it, can put down their roots in an alternative culture. Christianity is such a culture.

ibid

VIII *Thou Shalt Not Steal*

Thou Shalt Not Steal.   *Exodus 20. 15*

The Great Train Robbery of 1964 in Britain led to some
record sentences. There are men at this moment doing
thirty years for their parts in that multi-million mail hold-
up. In the same period very large sums of money, possibly
in the aggregate scarcely less huge, were being made by
respectable citizens out of real estate deals made possible
by enormously inflated land values. Yet one of these actions,
so far as the law is concerned, was theft. The other was good
business. Here is a paradox which makes of this eighth
commandment, which is concerned with social justice as
well as with the protection of property, a far more complicated affair than at first sight it appears to be. 'Thou
shalt not steal' ought to be simple enough. It ought to mean
exactly what it says, neither more nor less. And indeed,
in a sense it does. But if that were all, the commandment
would not be as important or topical as it is. Of the two
strands of meaning in it, one certainly represents nothing
more complicated than plain anti-theft legislation. Man
has sought to protect himself against the thief ever since he
came to possess private property, and has disliked the thief
and sought to restrain, frighten, and punish him: the
punishment often becoming more severe as society became
more fearful of its goods, a fact which the train robbers—
or those who were caught—learned to their cost.

Of course, protection from theft is a necessity, which
makes all the more grave the present virtual break-down
of law enforcement in this particular. For the first time,

crime is paying, fewer are being punished, and the professional criminal is doing very well. What is more, thieving is not only a danger to society; it is pernicious in its effects upon the thief. 'Let him that stole steal no more,' Paul wrote to the Christians at Ephesus, representing honesty as a necessary by-product of conversion. This, the conviction that personal honesty is involved with personal integrity, is an important ingredient in the making of character and self-respect.

The rot has set in once the belief has faded from many minds that stealing is *wrong*. All society has left then is more keys and more security measures, which is exactly what in fact is happening now, after a long period in which British honesty was the astonishment and admiration of the world. 'There is a feeling abroad,' said a writer in the *Spectator* not long ago, 'that fiddling and sharp practice are accepted as almost standard procedure in business, from the top executives of a big firm, who increase their private fortunes by phoney take-over negotiations, to the man on the shop floor who steals what he can in time from his employer. Why bother in an expense-account society in which everybody is in it only for what he can get out of it?'

It is easier to ask the question than to answer it. But that there should be an answer in the only place where it is useful to have one—the hearts and consciences of men— is beyond argument of critical importance. Honesty, after all, is part of a man's duty to his neighbour. So the first strand of meaning in this eighth commandment, the condemnation of taking what is not one's own, has relevance now, and more, not less, than in times gone by, when the Church Catechism was talking about 'picking and stealing,' instead of scrounging or knocking-off other people's property.

But a far more searching significance lies in the second

strand of meaning in the commandment—its concern with theft in the form of exploitation. The Church Catechism, in its heyday very much a property-owners' manifesto, conveniently makes no mention of this aspect of the matter. But the startling fact remains that the Old Testament, that quarry whence the commandment was dug, is far more concerned with theft in the form of exploitation than with theft in the form of breaking and entering. That craggy character the prophet Amos, with his burning sense of social justice, would have been more exercised about today's land value speculations than about the train robbers. 'They have sold the righteous for silver, and the needy for a pair of shoes,' he said of the wealthy of his own day, seeing in their general goings-on an affront to God, not only because they were rich but because of the lack of social responsibility with which they used the power and privileges of their wealth.

This second thread of meaning, therefore, is really concerned with social justice. It can be found gleaming here and there, very bright, in the enormous tapestry of the Old Testament. 'Thou shalt not defraud thy neighbour, neither rob him.' 'Trust not in oppression, and become not vain in robbery.' 'Rob not the poor because he is poor.' All can be summed up in the plain injunction: 'Thou shalt not steal.' But the kind of stealing envisaged is very different from the kind of thing which the Church Catechism had in mind. The villain of the piece, the oppressor, is almost always seen as the wealthy man, and it is worth asking, now that everybody's ambition seems to be to become one, why this should be so, and if there is anything in it.

The Bible in fact as a whole is very suspicious of 'riches.' A random collection of quotations on the subject makes interesting reading. They are seen as a snare and a delusion. 'Wise men die, likewise the fool and the brutish person perish, and leave their wealth to others.' They are seen as a cause of ulcers: 'The abundance of the rich will not suffer him to sleep.' They are seen as a barrier between man and God 'It is easier for a camel to go through a needle's eye, than for a rich man to enter into the kingdom of God.' They are seen as the cause of a false sense of security, as in Christ's story of the rich man who had accumulated, as he thought, enough wealth to see him through, and who was just beginning to relax when God told him that his soul would be required of him that very night. And, leaving the Bible and bringing the matter up to date, there is this, from D. L. Munby's book *God and the Rich Society*: 'The evils of riches, to the Christian, are the evils of distraction (the distraction that keeps men from thinking about God), the evils of a false dependence on the created order, and a would-be security that fails to take account of the inevitable fragility of human destiny on this earth.'

But always behind this general distrust of riches there is the implication that they are wrong in themselves whenever they involve indifference to poverty in others. So it is not wealth as such which the Bible sees as wrong—it sees it more as dangerous to the possessor—but the misuse of it. The possession of riches combined with indifference involves selfishness and exploitation; and these are not only forms of theft, but forms with which the eighth commandment is definitely concerned. It follows, therefore, that in any search for its meaning today, it clarifies the issue if the word 'steal' is replaced by the word 'exploit.'

This makes a world of difference. All sorts of things which we live with daily, as a fuzzy background to life, suddenly come into hard focus. Inflation, for instance, as a monetary policy, must involve injustice so long as it is blandly allowed to lead to the impoverishment of the elderly on pension, however much it seems to enrich those who are able to stay on the financial band-wagon. The blind drive for wage and salary increases without regard for the economic position of the country or for the needs of others, to take another instance, is a form of exploitation. All such modes of conduct do violence to the concept of social justice, however much we may hate facing the fact, or have to be dragged, kicking and screaming, to a realisation of it.

Nor are they the only ones. If the essence of theft is getting something for nothing, or at any rate trying to, many of the things we do today stand in need of examination. At the heart of much of our affluent-society thinking about making a way in the world is the notion that the smart man is the one who most successfully solves the problem of getting the most. Our whole way of life inevitably involves all of us at some time in some forms of exploitation in this sense. The trouble of late has been, however, that certain circumstances, operating simultaneously upon our lives, have, in quickening the pulse of getting and spending, raised the fever of exploitation to record levels. Obviously, something has gone wrong with money. It declines in value even as we look at it. And as this process continues, so more money is necessary to achieve the same results. We have to run harder in order to stand still. At the same time there are more goods and services to be bought, and therefore more temptation towards possession, so that a man can exhaust himself in the acquisition of gadgets. And always the H.P. man standeth at the door. The hire-purchase debt in Britain alone now stands at thousands of millions, and there are whole areas where to keep up with the instalments is the main object and exercise of life. But far more important has been the virtually unchecked growth of materialism in recent years. The attitude of mind involved—that material aims and needs are, in the last resort, all that matter—springs naturally enough from the decline in belief in anything beyond and behind this present world. Those to whom the future is a blank must needs value the present and its gratifications more than ever. We are all in this, every single one of us, and if this commandment can stir us even as far as an awareness of it, like an old tune touching a chord of memory of better things, so much the better.

Among the false gods we were looking at in connection with the second commandment was the hard-faced god of wage-packet and cheque book—Mammon. Here now, as we think about this eighth, we cross the border again into his restless kingdom where a man's worth is so often measured by what he possesses. That is one of the values of this world which we have invented for ourselves. But it is not a recent invention; the equation of wealth with virtue is as old as the hills, and the idea that God looks with especial favour upon the rich man, rather like a bank manager being benevolent towards someone with a big account, is one which has made a very deep penetration into the Christian Church.

> *The rich man in his castle,*
> *The poor man at his gate;*
> *God made them, high or lowly,*
> *And ordered their estate.*

The lines could be written in all innocence by the devout Mrs. Alexander, wife of a bishop, in her mid-Victorian hymn, wherein the state of affairs they portray is seen as yet another example of the divine plan which made 'all things bright and beautiful.' The fact is that there has been over the last few centuries a well-sustained attempt at a takeover bid by Mammon for the soul of Christianity. But the bid has never been wholly successful. Always, down the ages, there have been voices raised in protest—voices to take up the cry of Amos from so long ago: 'I will not turn away their punishment, because they have sold the righteous for silver, and the needy for a pair of shoes.' Let us try for a moment to trace some of these voices over the years. Ruskin, for instance, just over a hundred years ago, writing of the terrible consequences of the economic doctrines of Ricardo and Bentham in terms of the exploitation of cheap labour and other abuses at the coming of industrialism, could say: 'Nothing in history has ever been so disgraceful to human intellect as the acceptance among us of the common doctrines of political economy as a science. I know no previous instance of a nation's establishing a systematic disobedience of the first principles of its professed religion. The writings which we esteem as divine, not only denounce the love of money as the source of all evil, and as an idolatry abhorred by the Deity, but declare Mammon-worship to be the accurate and irreconcilable opposite of God's service.' That was in 1862, and the language was considered violent enough to embarrass the periodical publishing it. Yet who could say now, more than a century later, that the condemnation of economic exploitation which the words contain is not still justified and still relevant?

Then there was Charles Gore, in his day a famous bishop and thinker who, many years after Ruskin, was concerned with the same matter of social justice, and distinguished five ways in which the commandment 'Thou Shalt Not Steal' had meaning and punch. Some of his phrases may have now a dated sound. After all, he was writing before 1914. But they still bear heavily upon the conscience of anyone honest enough to expose the conscience to them.

The commandment is broken, he maintained, *by fraudulent dealings in business or trade, whereby our fellow man receives for money something less, or other, than he had a right to expect.*

In the modern scene, there are forms of fraud familiar enough in all conscience: goods below specification, bad workmanship, trick clauses in small print, dilatory payment for goods received, tax evasion, expense-account high living. The list, if prolonged, would be lengthy indeed.

The commandment is broken, Gore went on, by *'sweating' or requiring others to work for inadequate wages*.

The words might be immediately evocative of gas jets and pale workers of a day long past. But they also apply to such people as nurses in our day, whose sense of vocation we appear to be content to exploit and whose wages can be considerably less than those of a youth carrying bricks on a building site; or to primary school teachers struggling with vast classes for wages often less, as a fact, than those of typists. In an economy which appears to have no wages policy whatever, and where no one has solved the problem of relating worth and reward, such things may be bound to happen. But so long as they do it is idle to suppose that requiring some to work for inadequate wages is a thing of the past.

The commandment is broken, Gore continued, *by defrauding an employer of the best service of the employed*. This is surely not out of date. The sombre story of industrial conflict during recent years has involved rights and wrongs on both sides as between employer and employed. But it is just the plain unpopular truth that cases in which the employer, whether he has been private or public, has been sold short on the labour he was paying for, have been numerous and serious.

Fourthly, Gore maintained, this commandment is broken *by expecting others to work for us without doing our own fair share of work*.

Admittedly, there were more 'idle rich' riding on the backs of others then than now. Yet we ourselves are in many cases open to the same condemnation regarding our fellow men in the undeveloped countries of Africa and the East, upon whose labour and raw materials our economy still heavily depends. The emergent nations of black Africa may yet come to take their revenge upon us for this. We might not be idle; but by comparison with them we are very rich.

To quote Munby again, 'We need to be sensitive to the way that material possessions divide man from man and break up human fellowship. We need to be ready to use our abundance in common rather than for personal and private enjoyment. . . . Above all, we need to be aware of the mass of men living in poverty in the underdeveloped countries, whose condition we could do something to improve, if we were ready to make sacrifices ourselves on an adequate scale.'

Last of all, said Gore, the commandment is broken by neglecting the duty of *giving*. Some years ago a national daily started a lively correspondence by publishing the sorrows of a man who said he had difficulty in getting by on £5,000 a year. Many people wrote to demonstrate how they managed on a good deal less, exhibiting their domestic budgets to show how. The result was a significant revelation of the financial affairs of quite a number of families. Yet a fact which clearly emerged was that scarcely one of them budgeted for what Gore's age would have called 'alms-giving.' Clothes, cars, foreign holidays, food—the cost of these was worked out with impressive accuracy. But none whatever mentioned any giving. There was no heading, in fact, in any of the budgets, to suggest that such a category existed.

But this eighth commandment is indirectly reminding us, among so much else, that giving is important. For to be generous, to give of one's own for the help of others is as much a part of the practice of the Christian faith as prayer and worship, being an imitation of the divine compassion and a means of responding to the divine love by an exercise of love in return. 'Freely ye have received, freely give.' Conversely, non-giving is a form of theft in that it involves treating what is not our own as if it were, since we act then as proprietors rather than stewards of what God has given us. The harsh truth is that we have become involved in theft as soon as we have taken anything from the world and come to regard it as totally our own, to be used for our own personal ends of gain or enjoyment, without acknowledging the moral duty of sharing some of it with our fellows. To acknowledge that duty is to recognise at the same time the great truth that in fact we never really possess anything wholly; but only hold it as stewards, and then but for the short span of our lives.

One of the most convincing proofs of the truth of this lies in the quality of the individuals who, recognising it, have acted upon it. Always, throughout history, there have been those who, whether consciously as Christians or as generous-hearted men, have shown in their lives the essential nobility of the stewardship concept. Some of the most notable acts of giving have been Jewish, as the enormous benefactions of the Rothschilds bear witness. And an Oxfordshire man, Lord Nuffield, is yet more likely to be remembered for his princely gifts to medicine and the University of Oxford than for his automobile. Such have had many predecessors, even if on a lesser scale. There have always been those, like Henry Thornton, the evangelical business man mentioned by James Stephen in his essay on *The Clapham Sect*, who gave two thirds of his income to the poor throughout his life. 'Having inherited an estate which, though not splendid, was enough for the support of his commercial credit, he adjudged that it ought never to be increased by accumulation, nor diminished by sumptuousness: and he lived and died in the rigid practice of this decision. In the division of his income between himself and the poor, the share he originally assigned to them was nearly six-sevenths of the whole.'

High taxation might have made impossible now generosity on such a scale. Affluence for all, at any rate in the West, might have removed the poor from our own doorsteps to the streets of Calcutta, the African scrub, or the slums of Hong Kong. But the principle remains that nothing is in fact our own, that service is the rent we pay for our room on earth, and that theft in the sense of exploitation follows the forgetting of it.

After Gore, perhaps the next notable voice to speak out on this theme was Archibishop William Temple's. Since then, there has been little enough said. Maybe we have all been too busy getting better off: except the old, and the overseas needy. Maybe we could all benefit by beginning to think about it again. If so, this commandment will help.

'Thou shalt not steal.' An immense range of meaning is in fact spanned by the four words. For the commandment, far from being outdated, or reflecting only a simple concern with the protection of property, reaches out in fact into every corner of what R. H. Tawney called our 'acquisitive society.'

SOME QUESTIONS ABOUT THE EIGHTH COMMANDMENT

1. How many different kinds of theft can you think of?
2. Do you think crime pays? Have a good look at your answer. It might help you to answer the next question.
3. Do you honestly think honesty matters?
4. Looking around among people you know, would you say most were honest one hundred per cent?
5. How would you justify the view that stealing was wrong?
6. 'Thou shalt not defraud thy neighbour, neither rob him.' Can you think of actual instances of fraud being practised now?
7. 'It is easier for a camel to go through a needle's eye

than for a rich man to enter into the kingdom of God.'
Do you think this is true?

8. The Bible seems to think riches are dangerous to the possessor. Can you go along with this?

9. How do you feel about the effects of inflation on old people living on pensions? Angry? Indifferent? Or convinced no one can do anything about it?

10. Do you tend to admire rich people? If so, why? If not, why not?

11. How much of your income do you give away? A little? A lot? Nothing?

12. Do you feel this matters?

SOME THOUGHTS ON THE EIGHTH COMMANDMENT

What it Means

The (eighth) commandment is, Thou shalt do no theft, and included in the meaning of the same all wrongful usurpation of another man's goods, either by fraud, or guile, or by usury, or by violence, or by fear.

Law of John Peckham: Abp. of Canterbury, 1279

One Kind of Theft

My duty towards my neighbour is . . . to keep my hands from picking and stealing.   *The Catechism*

And Another

People today feel they are being got at from all sides, particularly by commerce. From morning to night they are bombarded by slogans and high pressure salesmanship. They get forced into buying things they don't want at prices they cannot afford. . . . These things are happening all the time and it seems they have no way of redress. Everything has become too large, too impersonal.

Article in The Times, quoted by Brian Inglis in Private Conscience and Public Morality

A True Word

Ay, sir; to be honest as this world goes, is to be one man picked out of a thousand.   *Hamlet*

Fair Question

Suppose you came into possession of money, belonging to somebody else, in circumstances where it was impossible they should find out that you had it. Would you keep the money if the somebody else was:

   (a) A relative?
   (b) A neighbour?
   (c) The local grocer?
   (d) The new supermarket?
   (e) British Railways?
   (f) The Inland Revenue?
   (g) A telephone call box?

If you decided to keep it in any of these circumstances, would you feel any qualm of conscience?

Brian Inglis: Private Conscience and Public Morality

The Plain Man Looks at the Commandments

If You Can Get Away with it

> *Thou shalt not steal; an empty feat,*
> *When 'tis so lucrative to cheat.*
>
> *A. H. Clough*

Beating the Tax-man

Tax avoidance, juggling with schedules, covenants, domiciles and beneficiaries, have made the accountant as important to the middle class family as a dentist or solicitor: avoidance is regarded no longer as a nasty trickery, but as a private duty.

Anthony Sampson: Anatomy of Britain Today

A Matter of Motive

Honesty is the best policy, but he who acts on that principle is not an honest man.

Archbishop Richard Whateley

IX Nothing But the Truth

Thou shalt not bear false witness against thy neighbour.

Exodus 20. 16

What is false witness? Various theoretical answers are
possible, such as that it represents the manipulation of
truth for a particular end. But the best way into the matter
is surely to have a look at some forms of it which can easily
be picked up, like different kinds of pebbles on the great
beach of life.

There is, for instance, the false witness of the garden-
fence reputation-poisoner. The ninth commandment is
intimately concerned with this sort of thing, and is broken
whenever gossip and slander damage lives, which they very
easily can do, and all the more so in proportion as the
victim is not strong enough to be indifferent.

Here is one of the commonest of all forms of false witness, about which few can be self-righteous, because most
are involved in it at some time or other. The tendency to
gossip about other people is a built-in human weakness. It
is also very old, and the Bible reflects the fact. 'Thou shalt
not go up and down as a talebearer among thy people,'
says Leviticus, rather hopefully in view of the fact that
most people do. Significantly, the writer of the 15th psalm
includes among the 'righteous,' 'he that hath used no
deceit in his tongue, nor done evil to his neighbour: and
hath not slandered his neighbour.' But who hasn't? This
must be the commandment most often broken: 'All of us
often go wrong,' St. James said in a remarkable passage:
'the man who never says a wrong thing is a perfect charac-

ter, able to bridle his whole being. If we put bits into horses' mouths to make them obey our will, we can direct their whole body. . . . So with the tongue. It is a small member but it can make huge claims. What a huge stack of timber can be set ablaze by the tiniest spark' (James 3.2-5).

Such is a general truth of human experience. Even so, this is only one kind of false witness; one pebble on the beach, and rather a small one at that.

A considerably larger one is a further kind of false witness which is concerned with what might be called the expert manipulation of facts. Some interesting examples of this can be picked up in the area of advertising. And insofar as this is done, such advertising comes under the condemnation of false witness. Not all does so, by any means. But that which does clearly comes within the area of meaning of the commandment, which includes the very large and growing realm of the mass-persuader in the modern world. What interested the framers of the commandment was basically the sinfulness of tampering with the truth for any end whatever. It therefore makes all the difference, and brings it instantly into the forefront of our concerns today if we change just a word or so in it, and for 'false witness' read 'propaganda.'

The commandment did not begin with so wide a field of reference. The fact that its relevance for today is enormously extended is only another instance of how almost all these principles seem to hold depths of meaning not only beyond general expectation, but also beyond the necessarily limited understanding of their original framers. This one, indeed, at any rate on the surface, represented little more than a reflection of the already existing truth that all societies have at all times feared and detested the liar. The Babylonian Code of Hammurabi, much older than the commandments, prescribed death for the false witness. In Roman Law, too, the principle was that he should be punished with the penalty appropriate to the crime of which he had wrongfully accused another. Later ages bored holes in the tongues of liars, or whipped them.

All societies have feared and punished falsehood, because all have known it as a dangerous practice. Unless the truth is respected in human affairs the basis of confidence is destroyed. The result can only be a free for all in which the biggest lie wins. And what makes the matter much more pressing now is the power of spreading falsehood which technology has placed within reach of those who wish to do that very thing. The resources at the disposal of the mass-persuaders are now immense, and so therefore are the consequences of the abuse of them, and there are many indications that these resources will become more powerful as time goes by. The discovery of increasingly formidable techniques of bringing persuasive influences to bear upon the human mind has gone a long way even in the last twenty years. The term 'brain-washing,' unknown before then, is commonplace enough now.

Here is a form of false witness in the sense of the deliberate manipulation of facts to achieve a particular end, infinitely more formidable than either of the other two. If those were pebbles, this is a boulder beneath whose weight truth itself can be crushed out of existence. It was a prophetic instinct for the shape of things to come which moved George Orwell in *1984* to give the name *Minitrue* to a ministry of propaganda concerned entirely with the distortion of facts to suit a given party line. This process was applied 'to every kind of literature or documentation which might conceivably hold any political or ideological significance. Day by day and almost minute by minute the past is brought up to date. . . . All history was a palimpsest, scraped clean and reinscribed exactly as often as necessary. In no case would it have been possible, once the deed was done, to prove that any falsification had taken place. . . .'

So here, then, are three possible kinds of false witness: malicious gossip, slanted advertising, ideological brain-washing. They could be identified as the domestic, the commercial and the political versions respectively of the same thing—the manipulation of facts to suit particular ideas. Of these three kinds, the first is very old; the last two comparatively new, and of greatly increased potential through a combination of psychological insights with means of mass-communication. If not brain-washing, at any rate brain-bending, is within the experience of most people now, and few get through a day without experiencing, through the mass of information coming at them from many directions, some degree of it.

But thus to identify and tabulate false witness is not the end of the matter so far as this commandment is concerned. For behind it lie two assumptions of the utmost importance: that truth is within human reach, and that it is enormously important. Both are necessary to the belief that the tampering with truth which false witness represents is not so much undesirable or tricky as positively wrong, a moral offence. The real question is, therefore, how true is either assumption?

Is truth within human reach? In times past man seemed to have little doubt that it was, and spoke of it with unbounded confidence. 'The inquiry of truth,' Francis Bacon wrote, 'which is the love-making, or wooing of it; the knowledge of truth, which is the presence of it, and the belief of truth, which is the enjoying of it, is the sovereign good of human nature.' 'Whoever knew truth put to the worse,' Milton asked, 'in a free and open encounter?' But there were always doubters as to whether truth, in the sense of conformity to fact, was a possibility.

Pontius Pilate, that civilised cynic, was expressing only the doubt of a man used to the ways of the world when, in answer to Christ's statement at his interrogation, 'My task

138

is to bear witness to the truth,' replied, 'What is truth?'
The question was rhetorical: so far as he was concerned,
there was no such thing. And in respect of truth as accuracy
of reporting, he would appear to have been right. We know
now that complete impartiality, as regards the description
of any event, is an impossibility. Always the report is col-
oured, either as to form or content, by built-in predilec-
tions, arising from the background, loyalties, and education
of the reporter. This point appears to have been missed in
the much admired and often quoted remark of C. P. Scott,
founder editor of the *Guardian*, that 'Comment is free:
facts are sacred.' That may well be so; but inevitably
reporting of the facts colours them. The difficulties involved in any historical writing make this plain. No history
can ever be 'true,' in the sense of being a precise and
accurate account of 'what happened when.' Reports of
identical events taking place in the world today would be
bound to differ fundamentally, according as they were put
out by Washington or Peking.

It may well be, therefore, that absolute truth in this
sense is beyond the capacity of finite human intelligence.
Maybe the possibility of making any wholly accurate statement is limited to the areas of dimensions and quantity,
when the statements can be arrived at by calculation, as
that two plus two makes four, or to reports of events without reference to causes. Thus a statement that a recon-
naissance plane was shot down over China can be verified
to some extent by a picture of the wreckage. Opinion and
tendentiousness creep in as soon as the occupants are
described either as spies or defenders of freedom, according
to the viewpoint of the reporters.

But if truth of this kind is so difficult of attainment, or
even impossible, a grave difficulty immediately arises in
the interpretation of this ninth commandment. If true witness is impossible, wherein lies the harm of false? If there

be no such thing as truth, what is there to stand between us and the view that the truth is merely what pays, or what the experts can persuade us to accept, or to regard as good for us at any given time? Without an answer to that, we are condemned to the smooth acceptance, as inevitable concomitants of modern life, of everything the mass persuasion experts care to produce out of the apparently bottomless store of their devices.

But there is another answer because there is another kind of truth: the moral quality of being honest to the facts insofar as we can see them, for all our acknowledged limitations at any given time. This is the kind of truth within reach and worth respecting because integrity is involved with it. This is the kind of truth which is prostituted whenever the mind is applied to the deliberate distortion of it. And that such is done every day, and is a familiar feature of the world we live in, does not make it any the less reprehensible or less dangerous. Falsification can reach a point at which not only will all truth be blanketed under clouds of propaganda, but where it can actually come to be forgotten that truth—even in the limited sense of truth as we know it—exists.

What, then, are the remedies? In terms of this world it is possible that there are only two, and that neither is satisfactory. One, adopted by some totalitarian states, is to impose complete control on all sources of information. The trouble here, as Orwell showed, is that where there is only one well of truth, it is easier to poison it. The other is to allow a great variety of sources of information to come together with virtually complete freedom of comment, as in most democracies. The trouble here arises from irresponsible use of such freedom. The point can easily be reached, and has almost certainly been reached now, when most people have a considerable degree of sales resistance to anything smacking, however faintly, of propaganda. Truth, as has often been said, is a first casualty in war, and the wars of this century have a lot to answer for, at this point as at others, for the general lowering of standards. Samuel Johnson put it well: 'Among the calamities of war may be justly remembered the diminution of the love of truth by the falsehoods which interest dictates and credulity encourages.' The difficulty is that truth cannot be played about with for a time, in the interests of this or that side in a conflict, without lasting damage to the idea of truth itself. Such damage has serious consequences. Not a little of today's cynicism, especially as regards politics, lies in the feeling, deep-rooted but by no means always well-founded, that politics in general are a lot of lies. Which then is worse, a state of affairs as in modern China, where the aim, as a deliberate policy, is for everybody to believe the party line; or the situation as in the West, where there is a predilection not to believe anything? The one makes leadership too absolute; the other any leadership more difficult. In either case truth is a casualty.

So both these purely worldly safeguards against false witness—control of sources of information, and the maintenance of many in the hope that they will be used responsibly, are neither really effective. The real remedy and the real safeguard must remain where it always has remained, in a deep reverence for the truth *as we know it*. We cannot get beyond that, although it may well be that more and better general education will win a slow victory over the forces of falsification by making more sophisticated our reactions to some of the absurdities which reach us now.

But education is not going to protect any of us from the possibilities of totalitarian control of all the information which reaches us, or from irresponsible tampering with it. The ultimate protection against any form of false witness is to be so in touch, in heart and mind, with a higher kind of truth than anything which this world affords, that distortions become apparent and the distorters themselves abhorrent. 'I will ask the Father,' Christ said, 'and he will give you another to be your advocate, who will be with you for ever—the Spirit of Truth. The world cannot receive him, because the world neither sees nor knows him; but you know him, because he dwells with you and is in you' (John 14.16-17).

It could be that the key words in this ninth commandment are the last three: 'Thou shalt not bear false witness *against thy neighbour.*' Here, at any rate, is a homely yardstick against which to measure the quality, in terms of truth, of anything we say, or come upon as said by others about others. How far is it helpful, how far is it impartial; or how far, on the other hand, is it loaded with innuendo or slanted towards a particular viewpoint? Such a simple test as applied, say, to our own talk in the course of a single day, or to the reporting of the world's news in the course of the same day, can have revealing results. One of them, oddly enough, is likely to be the discovery that though lies may shout from the housetops, there is, after all, such a thing as truth, and that it is, in this sense, within human reach and is still, because of its profound implications for all that we do and are, enormously important.

SOME QUESTIONS ABOUT THE NINTH COMMANDMENT

1. If false witness is the twisting of truth for a particular purpose, what is the first instance of it which comes to your mind?
2. Can you think of an example of false witness in the form of gossip?

3. Can you think of an example of false witness in the form of slanted advertising?
4. Can you think of an example of false witness in the form of political propaganda?
5. Which do you find the most serious?
6. Do you find anything wrong in the use of techniques of mass-persuasion?
7. War is said to be bad for truth. Can you think of any reasons why this should be?
8. Do you tend to believe what you are told, or not?
9. Would you regard brain-washing as a crime, a sin, or a useful way of dealing with an opponent?
10. 'Whoever knew truth put to the worse in a free and open encounter?' (John Milton). Do you think this to be still the case in the world today?
11. Do you feel that it matters?
12. 'What is truth?' (John 18. 38). How would you answer Pilate's question?

SOME THOUGHTS ON THE NINTH COMMANDMENT

Counsels of Perfection

Lie not at all, neither in a little thing nor a great, neither in the substance nor in the circumstance, neither in word nor deed: that is, pretend not what is false, cover not what is true.   *Jeremy Taylor*

It is unworthy of a Muslim to injure another's reputation, to curse anyone, to abuse anyone, or to talk vainly.
                                          The Sayings of Mohammed

The Plain Man Looks at the Commandments

Over the Garden Fence

> . . . *slander, meanest spawn of hell—*
> *And women's slander is the worst.*
>
> *Tennyson*

Whispered insinuations are the rhetoric of the devil.

Goethe

My duty towards my neighbour is . . . to keep my tongue from evil-speaking, lying, and slandering.

The Catechism

What the Serpent Said

All animals will one day remonstrate with the serpent and say: 'The lion treads on his prey and devours it, the wolf tears and eats it, but thou, what profit hast thou in biting?' And the serpent will reply: 'I am no worse than a slanderer.'

The slanderous tongue kills three: the slandered, the slanderer, and him who listens to the slander.

The Talmud

Another Kind of False Witness—Fact

—that a small army of well-educated people in advertising should believe that wrapping what they call 'mood' round a product is honest, makes me uneasy. At least, it can be argued, advertising is kept under constant scrutiny. But there have been many indications recently that the control exercised over it has been insufficient, notably in connection with cigarettes.

Caspar Brook, Director of the Consumers' Association, quoted by Brian Inglis in Private Conscience and Public Morality

144

Nothing But the Truth

And Yet Another—Fiction

Statistics were just as much a fantasy in their original version as in their rectified version. A great deal of the time you were expected to make them up out of your head. For example, the Ministry of Plenty's forecast had estimated the output of boots for the quarter as 145 million pairs. The actual output was given as sixty-two millions. Winston, in re-writing the forecast, marked the figure down to fifty-seven millions, so as to allow for the usual claim that the quota had been over-fulfilled. Very likely no boots had been produced at all. All one knew was that every quarter astronomical numbers of boots were produced on paper, while perhaps half the population of Oceania went barefoot. *George Orwell: Nineteen Eighty Four*

X The Itch to Possess

Thou Shalt Not Covet.   *Exodus 20. 17*

There was once a king in ancient times who looked out of
his palace window and saw something he did not need, but
yet wanted very badly. It was a vineyard belonging to one
of his subjects; a man called Naboth, who refused to sell.
The king was deeply upset. 'He laid him down upon his
bed, and turned away his face.' But he had a formidable
wife, this king, the infamous Jezebel, who in her husband's
name so fixed matters that a convenient political assassina-
tion took place, and Naboth was no more; and the vineyard became available to Ahab the king. However, before
he could take it over, Elijah the prophet, denouncing
what had taken place, passed on a message of divine
judgement which in the fulness of time was carried out.

Now of this famous old tale the subtlety lies not so
much in its detail as in its observation of the effect of the
itch to possess upon human character. The covetor is cor-
rupted. Ahab was by no means the last to be made miserable by the desire to possess something as a status symbol.
Even the lying on the bed and the turning away of the
face are significant, for there is the psychologically classic
picture of covetousness in action, destructive of content,
a gnawing envy. Just so, in the life of an individual,
might a man be made miserable—always provided that
possessions were his yardstick of the good life—by somebody else's greater wealth. Many do in fact suffer much
unhappiness from a sense of inferiority in material possessions. Covetousness as a problem is as important now—

probably more so—than when Naboth and Ahab and Jezebel acted out their sordid little drama.

So this last of the commandments is of the most profound significance because it 'strikes at the root and spring of all the evil in the heart of man. The region of our private thoughts and secret desires and hidden motives is the real stronghold of our rebellion against God. However fair a faith we may succeed in showing to the world, however correct our outward behaviour, there is that inner citadel, where the self, the ego, craves and envies and chafes, with the restlessness of the waves of the sea.'[1]

The trouble is that so much in the modern world encourages covetousness. Where the main motive of living is represented as getting, this is inevitable. The 'successful' man has over the last three centuries come to be seen, in the main, as he who has managed to acquire a lot of 'things'—land, houses, goods, and so forth. A man with two cars is deemed more successful than the man with one. Why should this be so? A very presentable argument could be made for the proposition that the really successful man, in terms of usefulness to his fellows, was the man who succeeded in possessing nothing, but in sharing everything. Such has certainly been the Christian ideal from earliest times, and those who have got somewhere near to achieving it seem to have been remarkably happy people. It cannot be entirely accidental that one of the outstanding characteristics of St. Francis was gaiety—the joyfulness of one who had put himself beyond the reach of covetousness by getting rid of such possessions as once he had. The contrast is sharp between such a man, happy in his voluntary poverty, and the sadness of the one who, as Mark relates, yearned to follow Christ, but was held back by his possessions. 'As he was starting out on a journey, a stranger ran up, and kneeling before him, asked: "Good Master, what must I do

[1] A. R. Vidler: *Christian Belief and this World.* S.C.M. Press.

to win eternal life?" Jesus said to him, "Why do you call me good? No one is good except God alone. You know the commandments: 'Do not murder; do not commit adultery; do not steal; do not give false evidence; do not defraud; honour your father and mother'." "But Master," he replied, "I have kept all these since I was a boy." Jesus looked straight at him; his heart warmed to him, and he said, "One thing you lack; go, sell everything you have, and give to the poor, and you will have riches in heaven; and come, follow me." At these words his face fell and he went away with a heavy heart, for he was a man of great wealth' (Mark 10.17-22).

The trouble here was not the possession of wealth so much as a mental blockage associated with it, inhibiting freedom of choice and action. Possessions had become so settled a preoccupation with a man otherwise of high principles as to handicap him fatally in the furtherance of them. Most of us are guilty in the same way; to touch our goods is to touch us on the raw. And the competitive society we live in, equating possessions with success, accentuates the process.

Nor is this true only in the life of individuals. Nations play this deadly game, too. Anyone who cares to contemplate the infamous story of the nineteenth century 'grab for Africa,' when the major European powers hurried to stake colonial claims for themselves in a whole succession of African Naboth's vineyards, can see to perfection the process of covetousness in action. And there have been plenty of examples since of the same thing. The seeds of many conflicts have been sown in these bouts of international coveting. The Congo today is just one of the long-term results. So, what the Bible means by coveting is essentially this itch to possess which is deeply embedded in human nature.

Herein—at this very point—lies the great challenge of this commandment. The other nine could at least be observed in the letter. This one needs to be observed in the spirit if it is to be observed at all. And since the desire to possess is fundamental to the acquisitive nature of man, it follows that the tenth is by a long way the hardest commandment of all to observe. The devout Israelite, or any of his Christian successors, who have acknowledged the authority of the commandments, could at least make a show of obeying most of them by not doing certain things, by not following certain courses of action. What was required was negative rather than positive. But this tenth offers no such loop-hole: for to obey this a definite change of mental attitude is required.

The commandment lists the goods which a man is not to covet, and the catalogue covers most of the goods which a man could possess in a primitive society, from a wife to the draught-animals of his establishment. But the original form of the commandment was: 'Thou shalt not covet.' In other words, 'Thou shalt not lust after anything at all.' That requires a literally superhuman effort to achieve, since it cannot be done by human will alone. This is the consideration which so overthrew Paul. In legal rectitude as regards the keeping of the Law as a true Pharisee he could, as he says in Philippians, fairly claim to have been faultless. As regards those commandments which required outward action he was in the clear. It was only when he came to the tenth that he made the staggering discovery not only that he was continually guilty of breaking it, but also that he was incapable, unaided, of amending his ways. 'For I know that nothing good lodges in me,' he wrote in Romans, '—in my unspiritual nature, I mean—for though the will to do good is there, the deed is not. The good which I want to do, I fail to do; but what I do is the wrong which is against my will.' So it was through recognition of his own inability to change himself in the fundamental manner which the commandment demanded that Paul was brought, through a highly involved psychological process, to realisation of his utter dependence upon the life-giving power of the spirit as revealed in Christ to release him from a bondage which was otherwise inescapable.

But the commandment could never have occupied such a position of importance in the spiritual and intellectual development of Paul had he not acknowledged, in the bent of mind with which it is concerned, one of the master sins. Why is this so? Covetousness, in so far as it can lead to envy and discontent, may well seem a highly undesirable attitude of mind. But it is certainly not immediately clear why it is a sin. What we have to discover, therefore, before this commandment can have much meaning for us now, is exactly of what the great evil involved in covetousness consists.

The answer, once again, lies with Paul. In Colossians he lists certain dispositions which need to be eliminated from the personality by all who, seeking to live in a new way in conscious discipleship of Christ, need to die to what they were before and to be reborn into an entirely different mode of life. 'Put to death,' he says, 'those parts of you which belong to the earth—fornication, indecency, lust, foul cravings, and the ruthless greed which is nothing less than idolatry.' There is the vital clue. Covetousness is evil just because it is idolatry, because it causes us to worship a whole array of false gods. No life can be other than mutilated which has as its main purpose the mere acquisition of more and more goods. For one thing, such a life becomes extraordinarily narrow in its horizons, which tend to stretch no further than self-interest can see. And, for another, such a life becomes essentially mean because it is inward-looking, concerned only with the satisfaction of personal ends. Covetousness is the deadly enemy of generosity, of selflessness, of such life-giving concepts as compassion and service of others. And somewhere along the road from covetousness lies the great grey granite city of Materialism, where most of us live now, and there the citizens accept with little question the depressing dogma that what really matters is how much a man possesses of this world's goods.

The degree to which the outlook and values of covetousness have penetrated modern life is very striking. A world which produces, as ours does, more and more goods to covet, and lives, moreover, by an economy which depends upon the selling of them to keep its wheels turning, is almost bound to be a place where the itch to possess is constant. Not all possession is wrong. Where it goes wrong is when it becomes the be all and end all of life. For the state of affairs has been reached then in which a man's goods are the things which he owns, and in which his highest aspirations are directed towards the ownership of some more, in flat contradiction of Christ's words: 'Be on your guard against greed of every kind, for even when a man has more than enough, his wealth does not give him life.' Slowly, gradually, and insidiously over the years there has crept into our culture an idea of progress which is almost entirely material in its nature. And the point of origin of the whole thing is the disposition towards covetousness built-in to human nature.

But what can we do about it? The last of the commandments does not offer any way out. Left to stand by itself it is almost entirely negative. No one is likely to become less covetous merely by telling himself that he ought to be. A far stronger medicine is required. The only hope is to change the mind itself. And that, as Paul discovered, requires a power greater than anything which resides within the self.

The trouble with any solely outward keeping of the commandments is that obedience to them can represent little more than an act of repression, which is likely to have the usual unhappy consequences upon the personality. Thus a man may not actually commit adultery; but he is still breaking the commandment if the desire to do so burns within him. A man may not actually steal, or commit violence against his neighbour; but he is still breaking the commandments concerned so long as he looks enviously upon his neighbour's goods. This was the essence of Christ's reinterpretation of the commandments—the revelation that it is the inner disposition rather than the outward act which counts. And so with covetousness; the way out is by replacing the itch to possess, with the active principle of disinterested love for all men which can be found in the conscious imitation of Christ. This is not some vague ideal. Obedience to the tenth commandment does not require an other-worldly indifference to material possessions so much as a refusal to see in them the sum total of everything. He who can manage to keep this commandment is emancipated rather than enslaved; is released from the rat race of getting and spending into the larger liberty of one who, having learnt to say 'enough is enough' in the face of the modern world's endless temptations to possess and to acquire, has thereby left a space in his life for service of God and man.

'This is one of the Master's sayings that brings you up against big things with a bump,' Studdert Kennedy said in *The New Man in Christ*, ' "Do not store up for yourselves treasure on earth, where it grows rusty and moth-eaten, and thieves break in to steal it. Store up treasure in heaven, where there is no moth and no rust to spoil it, no thieves to break in and steal. For where your wealth is, there will your heart be also."

'It seems at first a hard saying,' he went on, 'as though he were telling us that this world is no good except as a preparation for the next. Nothing in this world lasts. It all passes away, and therefore if your heart be set upon it all you will get, in the end, will be a broken heart. Death, the great thief, will break in at last and steal all away. There is deep truth in that.'

SOME QUESTIONS ABOUT THE TENTH COMMANDMENT

1. What do you understand by covetousness?
2. How far is your happiness dependent upon your possessions?
3. Do you find yourself envious of other people's possessions?
4. Success is often measured by wealth. Do you find anything wrong with this valuation? If so, what?
5. The modern world is said to encourage covetousness. Do you agree?
6. Can you think of some actual examples of this?
7. Which of your possessions could you most easily do without?
8. Why don't you?
9. What, in your view, if anything, is really *wrong* about covetousness?
10. St. Francis, who possessed nothing, seems to have been much happier than some of the world's very rich men. Can you offer any explanation of this?
11. 'Be on your guard against greed of every kind' (Luke 12. 15). What particular dangers was Christ warning against?
12. Do you see any connection between covetousness and the 'rat-race' of getting and spending?

The Plain Man Looks at the Commandments

SOME THOUGHTS ON THE TENTH COMMANDMENT

Words of Wisdom

Avarice breeds anger and blind desires, and is the fruitful mother of a countless spawn of sin.   *Hindu saying*

What does it matter how much you have? What you do not have amounts to far more.   *Seneca*

No Longer Fashionable

My duty towards my neighbour is . . . not to covet nor desire other men's goods; but to learn and labour truly to get mine own living, and to do my duty in that state of life, unto which it shall please God to call me.   *The Catechism*

The Acquisitive Society

> *The world is too much with us; late and soon,*
> *Getting and spending, we lay waste our powers,*
> *Little we see in Nature that is ours;*
> *We have given our hearts away, a sordid boon!*
>   *Wordsworth*

The man who covets is always poor.

Claudian

The Itch to Possess

Keeping Up With the Joneses

The assumption is that the attainment of material riches is the supreme object of human endeavour and the final criterion of human success. Such a philosophy, plausible, militant, and not indisposed, when hard pressed, to silence criticism by persecution, may triumph or may decline. What is certain is that it is the negation of any system of thought or morals which can, except by a metaphor, be described as Christian.   *R. H. Tawney*

You Can't Take it With You

What do superfluous riches profit in this world, when you find in them neither a succour in birth nor a defence against death? For without a covering are we born into the world, without provision we depart hence, and in the grave we have no inheritance.   *St. Ambrose*

The Ten Commandments of God

These are the holy commaundements ten,
Which God oure Lorde gave so strately,
By Moses his servaunte, unto all men,
Upon the hygh hyll of Sinai.

Thou shalt have none other God but me;
Set thou thy trust in me alone;
Love and dred me unfaynedly,
With harte and mynde at all season.

Thou shalt not take my name in vayne,
But call on it in all thy nede:
From othes and lyes thou shalt refrayne,
That my name be not dishonouréd.

The Saboth day halowe thou to me,
As I rested fro my workynge:
So cease thou from all vanite,
That I maye worke in thee all thynge.

Honoure thy father and mother also,
With men that are in auctorite:
Obeye them all, where ever thou go;
So shall thy lyfe be longe truely.

Thou shalt not kyll, nor hate any man,
Nor yet bear malyce in thy mynde.
Do thy enemyes the best thou can,
And to all men se thou be kinde.

Epilogue

Thy wedlocke shalt thou kepe truly,
And keepe other men to do the same;
That whordome and dishonestie
May be destroyed and put to blame.

Thou shalt not steale thy neighbour's good,
Nor get it with false marchaundyse;
But worke with thyne hands to get thy food,
And to sustayne the poore helplesse.

Against no man beare false witnesse,
And speake no evell to hurte his name:
Byt yf he fall thorowe his weaknesse,
Do thou thy best to cover his shame.

Thou shalt not thy neighbour's house desyre,
His wyfe, servaunt, nor mayde also;
But shalt be glad his good to forbeare,
As thou thyselfe woldest be done to.

Miles Coverdale (*1488-1568*)

Index of Biblical References

Index

The Author

William Purcell is a Canon Theologian of Coventry Cathedral, and the author of several books: *Pilgrim's Programme*, *This Is My Story*, *Onward Christian Soldier* (the biography of Baring-Gould), *Woodbine Willie* (the biography of G. A. Studdert-Kennedy), and the Fontana *The Plain Man Looks at Himself*. For the last ten years he has been engaged in Religious broadcasting and Television. He is married, with three children.